Practical Implementation
in Social Work Practice

Practical Implementation in Social Work Practice

A Guide to Engaging in Evidence-Based Practice

JENNIFER L. BELLAMY
and
DANIELLE E. PARRISH

OXFORD
UNIVERSITY PRESS

OXFORD

UNIVERSITY PRESS

Oxford University Press is a department of the University of Oxford. It furthers the University's objective of excellence in research, scholarship, and education by publishing worldwide. Oxford is a registered trade mark of Oxford University Press in the UK and certain other countries.

Published in the United States of America by Oxford University Press
198 Madison Avenue, New York, NY 10016, United States of America.

Library of Congress Cataloging-in-Publication Data
Names: Bellamy, Jennifer L., author. | Parrish, Danielle E., author.
Title: Practical implementation in social work practice : a guide to engaging in evidence-based practice / Jennifer L. Bellamy, Danielle E. Parrish.
Description: New York : Oxford University Press, 2020. | Includes bibliographical references and index.
Identifiers: LCCN 2019056844 (print) | LCCN 2019056845 (ebook) | ISBN 9780197509722 (paperback) | ISBN 9780197528228 (epub)
Subjects: LCSH: Social service, | Evidence-based social work.
Classification: LCC HV40 .B45 2020 (print) | LCC HV40 (ebook) | DDC 361.3/2—dc23
LC record available at https://lccn.loc.gov/2019056844
LC ebook record available at https://lccn.loc.gov/2019056845

1 3 5 7 9 8 6 4 2

Printed by Marquis, Canada

CONTENTS

Preface vii

Acknowledgments xi

1. The Three Circle Model of Evidence-Based Practice 1
2. The Steps of the Evidence-Based Practice Process 10
3. Evidence-Supported Interventions 26
4. Shopping for an Evidence-Supported Intervention 34
5. Implementation Overview 61
6. Adaptation and the Internal Logic of Interventions 89
7. Identifying and Defining an Adaptation Problem 101
8. Intervention Adaptation Models and Example 113
9. Fidelity 127
10. Conclusion 144

*Appendix A: Recommended Textbooks on Assessment and
   Evidence-Based Practice* 151
Appendix B: Evidentiary Checklists 153
Appendix C: Glossary 155
References 157
Index 163

PREFACE

The evidence-based practice (EBP) movement has emphasized the need for social work practitioners to use research to inform clinical decision-making and work to ensure that clients receive the best available, most effective services. Over this time we have noticed a shift in the narrative around EBP in social work. Although some spirited discussions continue to emerge about whether EBP is appropriate for use in social work and its allied fields, the conversation has largely turned away from "Should social work use EBP?" to "How can social work improve the quality of EBP?" And, happily, the tools and technology available to support the use of EBP in practice have improved a great deal in the last couple of decades.

For example, it is a whole heck of a lot easier these days to find research. Full-length articles may still be tough to track down, especially if one is not formally affiliated with a university, and many practitioners quickly grow bored, or maybe even panic, at the mention of methods sections and statistics. However, most research is available online. Gone are the days of wandering through the stacks of the library to find the actual bounded book that contained Volume X, Issue Y of Journal Z. We spent a lot of time in the stacks of real-live libraries—the physical library, in person, with actual books with pages you might thumb through. In the bad old days of library research, article abstracts were not easy to find through electronic databases. Based on the title alone one would attempt to hunt down a specific article only to find that some other student didn't return Volume X, Issue Y of Journal Z to its proper place on the shelf. It is a little disheartening to think how many hours we spent on these activities—never mind the expensive copy card charges, broken Xerox machines, iridescent lighting, and other irritating elements of the research process at the time.

Today, we have online search engines, databases, interlibrary loan service, and copies of manuscripts available to us before they are even in print. In other words, we can get our hands on a wide array of research from our personal computers, tablets, or smartphones. Even better, have clearinghouses, registries of evidence-supported interventions, and systematic reviews—all of which are efforts to gather the research evidence in a comprehensive way, assess its quality, and make it more accessible.

The increasing availability of these resources means that someone else, ideally an expert in the area, has already meticulously searched for and slogged through that research, ultimately producing a critical summary of the existing research evidence. This is a huge benefit to social workers striving to use research evidence in practice. Practitioners typically have little time to dedicate to finding and reviewing research. They also often have limited training in research appraisal. We are not saying that social work students don't get training in research methods and how to appraise studies, but there simply is not enough time in a typical two-year master's program to engage deeply in these skills. Research methodology is hugely diverse and also constantly evolving. The research designs and methods we learned as master's students do not represent the wide array of approaches that are used in the field today.

Over the last 20 or so years of the EBP movement, a lot of textbooks have been developed to motivate and train social workers in the use of the EBP process. We view EBP as a process through which practitioners identify a practice question, search for research evidence, critique the quality of that research evidence, implement practices based on their assessment of the evidence along with other important factors, and evaluate the result. There are books that describe how to search for evidence. There are even more books that describe how to understand, employ, and critique research methods in social work. There are books dedicated to client assessment and others that explain how to evaluate social work practice. We also note a number of books that describe a variety of interventions for particular problems or populations that are supported by research evidence. These are all important aspects of the EBP process. However, we felt that there were not any practical texts designed to help social work practitioners through the process of implementing evidence-supported interventions.

This book is meant to be an accessible resource for social work practitioners and students who want practical guidance on how to implement high-quality interventions in social work practice. We draw on research on EBP and implementation science in social work and allied professions. Although implementation is a relatively new area of research, there is a growing body of work in the area. Most of the work to date is highly technical, often written for researchers, and not generally framed from a social work perspective. While we ground the book in research, we also draw on our collective and practical experience. For many years now we have taught master's level social work students how to engage in the EBP process and have provided training on the process to social work professionals in the field. We have also developed and tested evidence-supported interventions for children, youth, and families. Likewise, we have experience working in partnership with agencies in the community and helped them with the evaluation of programs and interventions. This experience serves as another source of knowledge, as well as a pool of illustrations and examples that we use to clarify concepts and processes.

The new tools designed to gather and assess research evidence have improved a great deal with technology and are likely to continue to expand and improve. These efforts make research evidence much more accessible to social workers. We also currently benefit from a much larger array of high quality, evidence-supported interventions (ESIs) and intervention studies in social work and the allied professions than was the case 20 years ago. There are definitely gaps in the research. Unfortunately, many marginalized groups, including native communities, transgender folks, older adults, rural communities, and other groups are not well represented in existing research and even worse, have been exploited by researchers. We hope to openly acknowledge these problems and use implementation concepts to think about how to address them. Many times the students we work with pursue research papers to find out how to help the clients they serve only to be disappointed that there is very little high-quality research. Their first instinct is to switch the topic of their paper. We think it's important that they stick with it and grapple with how to use imperfect research, or research that is informative but not a perfect fit, just as social work practitioners are committed to working with their clients regardless of the state of the evidence base.

Just as there are gaps in research that is inclusive of particular populations and communities, there are gaps in the types of social work practice for which ESI have been developed. For example, there are more ESIs available for micro-level practices as compared to macro-level interventions. Some of the same principles and considerations apply to all levels of social work practice, and certainly those who work at the community or policy level will benefit from understanding how practices are carried out at the client, family, or local community level. Although this book will primarily focus on those practices that are carried out by social work practitioners working at the micro level, EBP broadly and implementation specifically are often framed as organizational processes or system processes. It's difficult for an individual social worker working alone in private practice to fully engage in EBP. There are fewer opportunities to share the burden in time, cost, and effort required to carry out each step of the EBP process. The one exception to this would be if the individual practitioner were part of an external EBP group or team, where there were shared efforts and resources and perhaps even opportunities to refer out for interventions they were not able to provide themselves. Therefore, we frame this book principally for social workers carrying out their work in teams and organizations who are seeking to identify and implement clinical ESIs on a larger programmatic or organizational scale.

The work of translating research findings into actual practice, on the ground, with real-live clients is challenging for a lot of other reasons. Research is often equivocal and hard to pin down. For example, a lot of social work students we work with are currently interested in mindfulness-based interventions. If they want to know whether mindfulness-based interventions work, the answer is: it depends. It depends on the outcome they hope to achieve, the age of their client, client language and culture, the qualifications and training of the provider, and a whole lot of other stuff. The existing research on whether mindfulness-based interventions work will not make clear on its own whether any given social worker should use it with the client in front of them or whether their agency should spend the time and money to get everyone trained in this particular type of intervention. Moreover, they will need to consider if those who would be providing this intervention are committed to learning and implementing this intervention as intended and investing the resources needed to sustain it over time. These practical considerations and challenges are the focus of this book.

If EBP is only in its adolescence in social work, then implementation is still in its infancy. You can think of interventions as "seeds" and the practice environment in which we hope these seeds will be used as "fields."[1] Federal and state governments and foundations have invested a great deal of time money developing, testing, and trying to get people to use seeds, but very little time and money learning how to plant these seeds into the fields where there is the proper climate and conditions for them to grow and sustain themselves. Social work master's programs tend to teach students how to find and assess the research that produce these seeds under ideal conditions as well as the foundational clinical skills required to learn how to deliver them. However, seeds that are not well nurtured are stunted, if not wasted. After all of the time and effort put into developing these ESIs and their potential promise to best serve clients, it would be a shame not to nurture them to their best potential.

[1] Credit to Dr. Ramesh Raghavan, Rutgers University for sharing this analogy.

ACKNOWLEDGMENTS

I would like to first acknowledge the huge influence Dr. Edward Mullen had on me and my work in evidence-based practice. He was a man before his time in terms of his ability to see the potential to use research evidence in social work practice before there was the technology and science in place to make the evidence-based practice process feasible. I am ever grateful for his mentorship and my great luck to have been his student. I would also like to acknowledge Allen Rubin, who gave me the opportunity to work with him through the process of book development and, in turn, gifted me the experience and confidence to work on this text. Also, I want to recognize David Follmer, who was encouraging, patient, and persistently positive that I could complete this project. It is also important for me to say how this book would not have been possible without the students, colleagues, community partners, and scholars whose contributions together form the content and purpose of this book. Writing these chapters made me think fondly back on all of the classes, studies, and partnerships from which I have had the benefit of learning over the years. Thank you, Danielle, for being one of those colleagues and helping to bring this work over the finish line. Finally, I want to thank my family for their patience and ever-present support, especially my husband Gene. I would not be in a position to do the work I do were it not for you, and I will never be able to adequately express how thankful I am.

—Jennifer L. Bellamy

I would first like to thank Jennifer Bellamy for the invitation to join her to collaborate on this book. I have great respect for her work, and it was truly a joy and honor to collaborate with her on a topic we are both so passionate about. I'd also like to thank my husband, Reuben, for his generous, selfless support, and both he and my daughter, Zoe (and the rest of my family), for bringing me so much joy and inspiring me to do work that I hope will make the world a better place. There is nothing better than a generous mentor, and I've been fortunate to have many who have supported me and taught me the ropes of both practice and research and the integration of them—Dr. Allen Rubin, Dr. Mary Velasquez, Dr. Kirk von Sternberg, Dr. Beth Pomeroy, Dr. Fred Childers, Dr. Mark Hanna, Dr. Debra Harris, and Al Grasso. My deepest appreciation to my mentors who have taught me so much and believed in me. Finally, I want to thank the many students and practitioners who have taught me so much about the challenges and potential for bridging the research–practice gap through research collaboration, training, and class. I look forward to continuing these discussions and learning from you as we work together to improve the lives of the people we care deeply about helping.

—Danielle E. Parrish

The Three Circle Model
of Evidence-Based Practice

This book is about how to best implement high-quality interventions in social work. If you want to understand intervention implementation, we believe it is important to understand evidence-based practice (EBP). From our viewpoint, implementation is a critical part of EBP in social work. When we ask social work practitioners and students what EBP means to them, they often say something like, "only using interventions that are shown to work" or "evaluating practice." The use of evidence-supported interventions (ESIs) is just an element of EBP. If you think too narrowly about EBP only as an ESI, you are robbed of the flexibility and reflection in action that is critical to good social work practice. Good social work is more than just following training, instructions, and manuals to carry out specified intervention. Professional social workers, by contrast, must make nuanced decisions about the judicious use of research in practice.

Imagine you are a brand new social worker, and you start work in an agency that serves older adults with chronic health problem–related depression. Let us also say that your supervisor would like to better serve the immigrant and refugee clients who are increasingly seeking services at your organization. You will likely find that there are some interventions that have been designed for and tested with older adults with mental health problems, others that have been tested with immigrant groups, and others for folks with chronic health problems. You may find nothing at all for refugee groups. ESIs haven't been developed for every single social work context, problem, or population subgroup. In this situation, you may decide to choose a depression treatment, like cognitive-behavioral therapy because it has a great deal of research evidence to support its use with a variety of populations. Or, you may seek to adapt cognitive-behavioral therapy to better fit your clients. Or, you might decide to borrow elements from a variety of interventions to construct a program. Or you may work closely with the community you want to serve to develop something completely new. Any one of these approaches, alone or in combination, are reasonable depending on the circumstances. How do you use EBP to decide? Each strategy takes careful consideration of a variety of factors that we will explore in detail throughout this book.

Evidence-Based Practice: From Medicine to Social Work

We think it's important to start with some background on the history of EBP broadly and in social work. The concept of EBP was first developed by physicians at McMaster's University in Canada in the mid-1990s (Sackett, Richardson, Rosenberg, & Haynes, 1997; Sackett, Rosenberg, Gray, Haynes, & Richardson, 1996). At the time, several studies indicated that physicians commonly used interventions that were outdated, or even harmful to patients, and that physicians relied on training that they received many years in the past. It was pretty disturbing. Imagine going to your doctor for treatment for a life-threatening condition and receiving an intervention that was based on 5-, 10-, or even 20-year-old knowledge despite the emergence of many new and promising treatments.

The physicians who originally conceptualized the EBP process did so to address this gap that had been identified—the gap between the best available medical knowledge and what was actually in common knowledge and use in medical practice. Their solution was the development of EBP as a specific *decision-making model*. In medicine, EBP was defined early on as "the conscientious, explicit, and judicious use of current best evidence in making decisions about the care of individual patients" (Sackett et al., 1996, p. 71). This definition has evolved over the years, both in medicine and in social work, as well as other disciplines. The core idea has remained. The very best available research should be considered when choosing an intervention. In the field of social work, and in this book, an *intervention* refers to any technology, program, practice, or policy designed to change targeted outcomes for clients. Clients may be served at any level of practice including individuals, groups, families, organizations, communities, states, and even countries. Although the focus of this book is on clinical practice in social work, which reflects where most ESIs in social work have been developed, many of the principles and ideas can be translated to community and macro practice as well.

We want to pause here to highlight a couple of things. First, EBP was developed in medicine and not social work, and the original terms and concepts were aimed at guiding the practice of medicine and therefore were not a perfect

---

Box 1.1

"In medicine, EBP was defined early on as 'the conscientious, explicit, and judicious use of current best evidence in making decisions about the care of individual patients.'"

---

fit for social work. Medical practice is similar to, but distinct from, social work practice in ways that can influence the EBP process. Many social work critics of EBP point to the more "messy nature" of problems addressed by social workers, the lack of resources available to social work practitioners, and the high value social work places on relationships as a foundation for intervention. Medical professionals and medical research may more often focus on the treatment of a single diagnosis or a specific part of the body, and many physicians are only able to spend a few minutes with each client. Social workers often work with clients on a variety of problems, and we aim to bring an ecological approach to our work. In early EBP models, individual practitioners were directed to pose a specific treatment question for each client, consult the research evidence, select an intervention, and implement the intervention. This process begins to feel overwhelming when clients have multiple presenting problems, many of which are not only the result of physical problems alone, but also complicated social, historical, and environmental processes. Social workers need not only to intervene with an individual intervention but also work to advocate for more progressive policies. As social workers, we bring a social justice approach to the work as directed by the National Association of Social Workers (NASW) Code of Ethics (National Association of Social Workers, 2017), whereas the Code of Medical Ethics of the American Medical Association emphasizes serving patients first and foremost (American Medical Association, 2016).

The complexities of social work and differences between social work and medicine can present challenges to engaging in EBP but are not strong arguments against the core principle of using the best available research evidence to guide practice. Using the best available research evidence to inform social work practice is a social justice mandate. If we align our work with the NASW Code of Ethics in that social workers seek to serve and empower the most vulnerable communities and we agree that research evidence is a resource to which vulnerable populations should have equal access, then a failure to use research evidence to bring the best interventions possible to vulnerable communities compromises our social justice mandate.

Shortly after EBP emerged in medicine, social work scholars began to apply and adapt the model to better fit social work practice. Scholars like Edward Mullen, Eileen Gambrill, Leonard Gibbs, and others worked to translate the major concepts of EBP for social work practice. Although the EBP approach to the integration of research knowledge into practice was novel, the effort to use science to guide social work practice has been a part of the profession since its beginnings. Although many of the concerns about the fit between EBP and social work have been addressed as EBP was further refined and integrated into social work education and practice, challenges remain. We'll identify these challenges and discuss approaches to addressing them as we go along.

The challenges we face in our efforts to use research to provide the best services possible for clients and communities are the same as those that many disciplines are struggling with. Medicine, nursing, public health, psychology, and education are also all grappling with many of the EBP challenges described in this text. The history, roles, and values of each of our respective professions impact the way we understand and apply research, but there is benefit from the shared struggle as the professions communicate new knowledge and share ideas and potential solutions with one another (e.g., Bellamy, Spring, Mullen, Satterfield, Newhouse, & Ferguson, 2013). Social work has always been interdisciplinary in nature, and it is one of our clear strengths. Working across disciplines expands our thinking on how we might lessen the gap between research knowledge and practice, and by our observation, current trends in practice suggest increases in intraprofessional training, research, and service delivery.

If we start with the core concept that EBP is essentially the effort to use research evidence in practice decision-making, we can consider different models and approaches to achieving that goal. There are two dominant approaches to using research evidence in practice currently in use in the United States. We think it's also helpful to keep in mind that EBP is a relatively new model in general, and so models and approaches to EBP are likely to expand and evolve over the years. In this chapter, we will describe the first major model, The process model of EBP. In Chapter 3 (this volume), we provide an overview of the other dominant model, the use of ESIs.

Box 1.2

"Although many of the concerns about the fit between EBP and social work have been addressed as EBP was further refined and integrated into social work education and practice, challenges remain."

The EBP Process Model as Represented by the Three Circle Model

The EBP process model is the one we consider most comprehensive in what is sometimes called the six-step model or the bottom–up model of EBP. Moving research knowledge into practice is challenging, and doing so requires the consideration of multiple factors, which makes it complex. Although the EBP process model framed much of the early discussion on the use of EBP in social work and the allied disciplines and is the model most closely aligned with the original model of EBP developed in medicine, it is not the dominant approach used to integrate research into social work practice. Its complexity is both a strength and a weakness. The more complicated something is, the more difficult it is to disseminate widely. When practitioners are surveyed about whether they are using the EBP process model, they often report using parts of it, and only sometimes, in practice, but very rarely the whole thing (e.g., Parrish & Rubin, 2012). They are more likely to name the use of specific ESIs, like motivational interviewing, assertive community treatment, or Homebuilders*, as their approach to using research evidence in practice.

The EBP process model is often represented with three concentric circles, or a series of steps. Where the three-circle version articulates the components of the model, the steps guide the implementation of the EBP process model in practice. The three circle model highlights the sources of information that must be considered to formulate practice decisions as well as a set of values reflected in the model. Figure 1.1 includes a representation of the three circle model that was developed by a group of scholars across allied disciplines including social work, psychology, psychiatry, and nursing. Because each of these professions contributed to this particular representation of the EBP process, and therefore it transcends disciplinary boundaries, it is called the transdisciplinary model of EBP.

The best available research evidence is just one of the components of the model, represented as the circle at the top of the figure. Although research evidence is often the component of EBP that gets the most emphasis, it is balanced out by two other circles at the center of the model representing clients and resources. First, client characteristics, state, needs, values, and preferences are represented as another circle in the model. Information from and about the client is gathered from assessments and communication with the client about their strengths, needs, goals, and priorities. This would include interviews with clients, psychosocial assessments, case records, or other important sources of client information. If you are working at macro, community, or policy level, the parallel sources of information might be the use community needs assessments

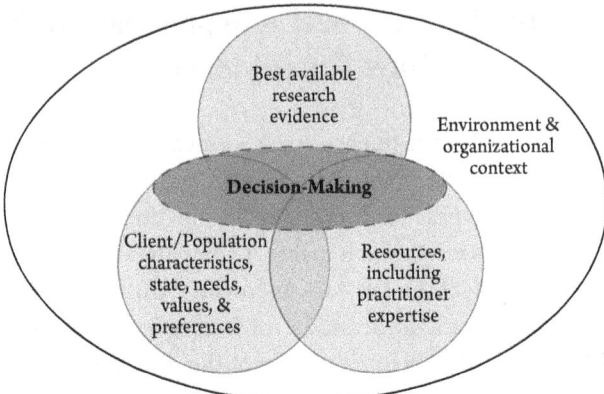

Figure 1.1 The transdisciplinary model of evidence-based practice. *Source:* Reproduced from J. L. Bellamy, B. Spring, E. J. Mullen, J. M. Satterfield, R. P. Newhouse, & M. Ferguson, 2013, Implementing evidence-based practice education in social work: A transdisciplinary approach. *Research on Social Work Practice,* 23(4), 426–436.

or other efforts aimed at understanding and engaging with the communities you hope to serve.

Research evidence may point to a particular intervention as the "best" in terms of achieving a particular outcome for the largest percentage of people, but if the client or community is not included in the process, the research doesn't fit their characteristics, or they do not buy in to the intervention, it's unlikely to succeed (Wampold & Imel, 2015). Unfortunately, social workers have too often assumed a role as an outside expert, entering communities of which they are not a member to provide interventions that have been developed and tested in other places with other communities. Social workers can offer research knowledge and information to clients, help communities select and implement interventions, or help communities develop their own knowledge interventions. If social workers foist interventions on clients without entering the relationship, they are exercising their power and privilege rather than empowering clients. Social workers should work to diminish the power differential between ourselves and our clients so that we work as partners in the intervention process (O'Neill, 2015). Clients and communities often reject interventions that have been placed on them, rather than co-developed or initiated (Castro, Barerra, & Steiker Holleran, 2010; Merzel & D'Afflitti, 2003).

The value of client-centered practice and client collaboration in the EBP process model is well aligned with social work values. Imagine working with a client who has a child with behavior problems and you are helping them to decide which parent training intervention they would like to use, our job as social workers is to translate the research for them so that they understand which models have

Box 1.3

"Research evidence may point to a particular intervention as the 'best' in terms of achieving a particular outcome for the largest percentage of people, but if the client or community is not included in the process, the research doesn't fit their characteristics, or they do not buy in to the intervention, it's unlikely to succeed."

been tested and shown effective for which outcomes and which populations. It is also our responsibility to talk with them about other elements of the intervention that may or may not be a good fit based on our assessment knowledge and relationship with the client. We need to understand the interventions that are available so that clients can have the benefit of this knowledge to help them make decisions for themselves. Some folks, for example, are going to like the individual-focus and technology involved in parent–child interaction therapy, an ESI for behavior problems. In this intervention, parents wear a "bug" in their ear so that they can be coached through interactions with their children. Others might prefer a group-based ESI that uses more discussion and videos, like the Incredible Years' intervention. Other parent training interventions may have less robust research evidence indicating their efficacy, but they may be specifically crafted for dads rather than moms, such as Nurturing Fathers. Fathers may choose this intervention instead, even we can't be as confident in the intervention outcomes. Even if we aren't able to offer a full array of intervention choices to our clients, as is often the case, it's our responsibility to be knowledgeable about them and share this knowledge with our clients.

Also included in the three circle model is a circle that represents resources. In this third resource circle, we are cued to think about what is feasible due to limitations in physical space, funding, time, knowledge, skill, staffing, or other practical limitations. Depending on the intervention, this can be challenging, as many social workers must work within many resource limitations. Budgets are tight. Caseloads are large. Timelines are squeezed. Even if the research evidence points to a particular intervention as having the most convincing research evidence, it may not work if you are not well trained in its use, you do not have the funding to provide it, or the limitations of time prevent you from using the intervention in full.

More recently, intervention developers and trainers are providing more tools to help practitioners assess whether they have the resources necessary to carry out an intervention correctly and completely prior to investing in training, manuals, or other intervention elements. In cases where this information is not easily found, it can be helpful to look for other organizations or practitioners who are actively using the intervention to learn what these resources are. This strategy can be helpful even if there is some readiness information provided. Your colleagues can speak from their perspective as fellow practitioners about their experience using the intervention, including any unforeseen challenges.

This example highlights another important value inherent to the EBP process model: transparency. Although social work practice has long been framed as a collaboration between practitioner and client, transparency has not always been practiced. Social workers and other allied professionals are often positioned as the expert who knows which intervention is best. In this model of EBP, however, it's the responsibility of the social worker to gather and translate information from all three circles for clients so that they are empowered as informed participants in the decision-making process. Clients may not be able to understand the technical elements of the research that may guide the decision-making process, but social workers can communicate these findings in an accessible way to help the clients understand the strength of the research evidence and the implications of those studies.

All three of these circles are situated within a wider context, including the agency or organization within which the services are provided. Just as we integrate our knowledge of research evidence with our knowledge of clients and their needs and preferences, so too do we integrate our knowledge of resources. In some cases, because of resource limitations you may only be able to realistically offer one intervention to a client. In this case, you should be able to clearly explain why this intervention was chosen given resource limitations and what the research evidence indicates about the intervention, including its alignment with client characteristics, needs, and preferences.

Organizations are located in the larger service context, which may be impacted by local, state, or even federal policies, licensing guidelines, funding structures, or other situational and historical factors that can influence how services are provided. In the social, political, and historical context of the writing of this textbook, Donald Trump is the president of the United States. Some funding streams for social programs have been cut. Others, such as investments in smart decarceration and interventions to fight the opioid epidemic, have

---

Box 1.4

"Although social work practice has long been framed as a collaboration between practitioner and client, transparency has not always been practiced."

increased. Increasingly harsh policies designed to track, dissuade, and detain immigrants and refugees are on the rise. A renewed sense of activism is emerging in the social work profession, as is a strong desire to do something, fight complacency, racism, and counter current threats to women, LGBTQIA communities, Muslims, and others. Social work practice is embedded in this context, and so too is EBP. Some interventions, although supported by research evidence, may not find community support our current times.

At the center of the EBP process model is professional decision-making. That was the crux of the original definition of EBP out of medicine, and it remains in the center of the current model. Research evidence doesn't tell you what to do. That's the difference between being a technician and being a professional. A technician can carry out the steps of a procedure using instructions. A professional must integrate information from a lot of different sources, make decisions about how to precede, evaluate how things are going on the fly, and make adjustments as needed. Social workers are professionals, not technicians. The EBP process model directs the social work practitioner to incorporate information from all of these circles together and give this information to the client to collaborate together to formulate a decision about how to intervene.

The transdisciplinary, or three circle, representation of the process model demonstrates how all of these elements are balanced to guide practice decision-making. Although helpful in articulating the elements of EBP and some of the values inherent in the process, this representation of the model doesn't really articulate how to proceed with this approach in practice. Therefore, the EBP process model is also often described as involving six steps (e.g., Sackett, Straus, Richardson, Glasziou, & Haynes, 2000; Straus, Richardson, Paul, & Haynes, 2005; Gibbs, 2003), which specify the process itself.

Discussion Questions

1. How is social work practice similar to and different from medical practice? How might these differences impact the use of evidence-based practice?
2. What social work values are reflected in the EBP process model?
3. How can social work address the barriers to improve the use of the EBP process model in practice?

The Steps of the Evidence-Based Practice Process

We want to start with a couple of notes about the evidence-based practice (EBP) process model before we describe each of the steps that describe how the process is carried out. First, this process was originally described in medicine as being carried out by an individual practitioner, whether that was a physician, social worker, nurse, or psychologist. In our experience, it may be more realistic for these steps to be completed as part of a team based on time, skills, or how on decisions about service delivery are made at an organizational level. Individual practitioners may not realistically have the time, training, or resources to engage fully in each of the steps of the process. Also, decisions about which interventions, policies, or programs are implemented may be made at a team, supervisor, or organizational level in many cases. Teams made up of individuals with the decision-making authority and resources needed to engage in the process; those with knowledge of organizational resources, client and community characteristics, and policy; and those expected to implement the intervention are better equipped to engage in the process together.

So, what to do if you are an individual practitioner without the benefit of a team or organization to support your use of the EBP process? In some ways, this simplifies things as you can proceed through the steps of EBP, including implementation, to suit your specific practice and process. You also might seek ways to share resources with other individual practitioners. You can seek out others who are interested in improving their practice in the same area and share training, materials, or supervision resources and form a partnership or informal group to reduce the burden and benefit from some of the advantages of a team. In our experience, there are many local groups that are organized around supporting work in a particular area. In Denver, where one of us is located, for example, there are groups designed to support evidence-supported work with fathers, home visiting, and many other populations and service systems. Moreover, advances in technology and the development of clearinghouses, reviews, and

---

Step 1: *Convert information needs into an answerable question.*

Step 2: *Track down the best evidence to answer the question.*

Step 3: *Critically appraise the evidence for its validity (closeness to the truth), impact (size of the effect), and applicability (usefulness in practice).*

Step 4: *Integrate the critical appraisal of the research evidence with resources, experience, and client*
characteristics, state, needs, values and preferences.

Step 5: *Implement the selected intervention.*

Step 6: *Evaluate the intervention.*

Figure 2.1 Steps of the evidence-based practice process.

systematic reviews make it more possible than ever to use the work of experts and other groups who have already reviewed and summarized the work. We'll discuss these resources later in Chapter 4 (this volume).

The Steps of the EBP Process

The EBP process generally includes six steps, which are outlined in Figure 2.1.

Step 1: Convert Information Needs into an Answerable Question

Although assessment is not always explicitly listed in the steps of the EBP process, an initial assessment of the client or community is needed to determine what questions and client characteristics are important in formulating an EBP question. The assessment should provide information about what the problem or goal is (including the clients' perspective on what they would like to work on and what they want from an intervention), as well as the factors that might impact the client's ability to engage in any services or how well those services might work for that client.

It's beyond the scope of this text to dive deeply into assessment, but we have provided a list of recommended texts on assessment in Appendix A. Here we review some basic pieces of information that are critical to include in the assessment process from an EBP perspective. For example, one thing we do know based on research evidence is that client buy-in matters. It matters for achieving the best possible outcomes, and it is critical from an ethical standpoint as well. Getting your client's perspective on what they see as the problem or goal is

---

Box 2.1

Getting your client's perspective on what they see as the problem or goal is important, whether your client is an individual or a community.

---

important, whether your client is an individual or a community. Oftentimes in social work we see clients with lots of problems and goals. Sometimes the tricky part is choosing where to start. You might ask what one, two or three problems or goals are most important to your client—either through an intake process, psychosocial assessment, or community assessment—and begin there.

The second thing you need to collect through assessments before you formulate an EBP question is basic information about your client including age, gender, race, ethnicity, language, socioeconomic status, and primary presenting problem or diagnoses. These are also pieces of information generally collected in basic psychosocial and community assessments. These are also the characteristics that can (sometimes) inform what intervention might be best suited for a client. We say (sometimes) because many intervention studies only answer the question: "Does the intervention work?" Fewer studies also examine the conditions and characteristics that are related to better or worse intervention outcomes. The reason that fewer studies look at this question is that intervention studies, particularly highly rigorous ones, are very expensive. One of us recently conducted a relatively small, basic, intervention study, which was funded at over $500,000 to complete. To answer research questions that relate for whom the intervention works and under what conditions require larger numbers of participants; and larger numbers of participants add expense. It's not uncommon for larger intervention studies to cost millions of dollars. However, if you do find studies that provide some insight into how well the intervention is likely to work for clients and communities such as those you serve, this information can be highly valuable in making decisions about which intervention might work best.

Once you have completed the assessment process, you can move on to formulate a specific EBP question. Remember, the client here could be an individual. But, the client can also be a couple, a family, a school, a state, or even a country. EBP was created for clinical practice, but the principles apply to macro level questions as well. So, you can use the EBP process to ask the question at a micro level: "If young first-time fathers are provided home visiting services, will they be less likely to use harsh parenting practices?" Or, you can use the EBP process to ask the question at a macro level: "If the state of Colorado provides home visiting to all young first-time parents, will the rate of child maltreatment be reduced?" Figure 2.2 provides some example of EBP questions that are focused at a variety of practice levels.

EBP process questions are unique in that they require specificity about clients, interventions, and outcomes. Oftentimes students and practitioners want to ask very general questions like, "What is the best service to provide to young parents?" The reason this type of general question does not work very well as an EBP question is because research studies aren't set up to answer the question, "What is the best service?" Intervention studies are designed to answer questions like "Does home visiting improve rates of breastfeeding initiation?" or "Does parent training reduce children's behavior problems?" Most often only one intervention is tested at a time with only a few outcomes. Sometimes you'll find studies that compare two or more interventions, but that is actually pretty rare.

We also need to be specific about the outcomes we hope to achieve because, sometimes different models or programs are stronger or weaker depending on the outcome. Many research studies find that an intervention works well for one outcome, but not another. So, one home-visiting program may be the best at reducing child maltreatment, whereas other home-visiting programs may be better at preparing children to enter school, and yet another is best for supporting health related outcomes like breastfeeding and healthy birth weight.

You also need to be specific about what intervention is being tested so that if we find that it works and we want to use it in practice, we can replicate the intervention more or less in the same way as it was used in the study. If an intervention isn't replicated more or less the same in practice as it was in the research study, the outcomes are less likely to be achieved. There are several examples where that's exactly what happened. Evidence-supported interventions that look impressive in studies sometimes yield disappointing results in practice.

If older adults are provided with meals on wheels services, will they have reduced risk for depression?

If people living in rural areas are provided with telehealth access to a nurse, will emergency room visits be decreased?

If schools serving low-income students provide breakfast and lunch service to students over school breaks, will students miss fewer days of school during the academic year? If first generation Asian immigrant adults are provided with culturally congruent health services, will participation in preventative health care visits increase?

If people living in a food desert are provided access to a community garden, will community cohesion be increased?

Figure 2.2 Examples of evidence-based practice questions.

Box 2.2

If an intervention isn't replicated more or less the same in practice as it was in the research study, the outcomes are less likely to be achieved.

This happened in the case of motivational interviewing (MI). There were some disappointing results in research studies related to this very popular, highly disseminated intervention. But, upon closer investigation, it turned out that practitioners were not implementing MI with a high degree of fidelity to the intervention. So, instead of MI, they were doing "marginally MI," "sort of MI-ish," or something else because they were leaving out important elements, changing them, and/or not employing the elements properly.

If you aren't sure about what interventions are out there, at this stage, it would serve you well to do a little searching to find out what your options might be. We find that many students and practitioners who are new to a particular area of practice are not familiar with current interventions. If that's you, some strategies you might use to find which interventions you might consider include:

- *Talking with colleagues about what they are using or have heard that others use.* Not only can your network of colleagues inform you about interventions, you all can use this strategy to get some informal information about how people like particular models, or other practical information like how burdensome the intervention is in terms of cost and time or how to access local training.
- *Contacting a research expert in the field.* Experts might be researchers or faculty at universities or research centers. Many university websites now provide search engines or other online lists of faculty organized by areas of expertise. A Google Scholar search can also reveal people who have written about the type of intervention in which you are interested, or who have published in the area. You can email an expert or request a quick conversation to learn about gold standard and new or developing interventions in the field. Other resources such as ResearchGate (https://www.researchgate.net/) can also give you access to download or request research papers directly from the authors.
- *Exploring conference websites or attending one yourself.* Conferences often represent the state of the art in the field and are a good source for identifying which programs and models represent the most innovative—even before they appear in journal articles or other publications. Conferences can also connect you to experts or colleagues that might be able to help.
- *Looking at registries, clearinghouses, or systematic reviews.* There a several websites that provide summary information about different interventions,

such as the California Evidence-Based Clearinghouse for Child Welfare. There are many other examples of such resources in mental health, substance abuse, medicine, and violence prevention. Also, the Campbell and Cochrane Collaborations publish systematic reviews, which review and evaluate the best available research evidence in different areas medicine and social interventions.

Step 2: Track Down the Best Evidence to Answer the Question

Once an answerable EBP question has been identified, a search plan to locate the best available evidence can be developed. In the early days of EBP, it was generally expected that individual practitioners would specify search terms and identify and critique each of the research studies they found. Over time, we have learned that this was too time consuming and not very feasible for busy practitioners when there was a large number of research studies. Also, not all practitioners were confident in their ability to critique the research. Fortunately, a number of organizations have begun to offer online resources that summarize this research, such as systematic reviews, clearinghouses, and registries. Some of these resources also offer additional information such as who to contact to get the intervention materials and the cost to implement the intervention to ensure its adoption is feasible.

A systematic review is a statistical synthesis of the available research that answers questions important to practice. These reviews are highly technical and can be expensive when done right. For this reason, these studies are usually conducted by teams of experts who engage in a detailed planning process, an exhaustive search and critique of research—including unpublished studies and studies in languages other than English—and the integration of findings across studies using statistical techniques. Several years ago, one of us attended a conference on systematic reviews and someone stated that on average these things take two years and $60,000 to complete. The average cost has increased since that time, but most practitioners do not have two years and $60,000 to painstakingly rummage through the existing research evidence looking for original studies. If there is any consistent finding across studies of the barriers to EBP in social work practice, it is that limitations in time and resources make this kind of exhaustive search of the research literature nearly impossible.

Two commonly used and respected organizations that offer systematic reviews are the Cochrane and Campbell Collaborations. They have processes in place to prevent bias that may emerge from conflicts of interest or commercial sponsorship of research. Such processes are important to keep the reviews objective and as unbiased as possible. These reviews are also routinely updated as new research emerges, which helps us to be aware of new approaches that may be more effective. The Cochrane Collaboration focuses more on health and mental health issues, whereas the Campbell Collaboration provides reviews more broadly on social interventions at and beyond the level of the individual. One example of a recent systematic review published by the Cochrane Collaboration was titled, "Psychosocial Interventions for Informal Caregivers of People Living with Cancer" (Treanor et al., 2019). If you go to the Cochrane Collaboration Library and search for this review, you'll find a "plain language summary," which provides clear, easy-to-comprehend findings and implications from this synthesis. In this case, this one-page summary details that 19 studies met the inclusion criteria and that these studies suggest that these psychosocial interventions do not impact outcomes for caregivers to a clinically meaningful degree. They also suggest that higher quality research needs to be done and that future intervention development should include caregiver input and pay attention to individual personal needs. Voila! This is so much faster than searching through all of the literature, critiquing studies for their scientific rigor and then making sense of the 19 acceptable studies by yourself. The Cochrane Collaboration also recently started releasing Cochrane Podcasts, where you can listen to a short summary of recent Cochrane reviews by the authors while sitting in traffic or taking a leisurely walk.

There are also a number of online clearinghouses and registries available that provide detailed information about empirically supported interventions, often with tools and contact information for their adoption. Some examples of these will be provided in Chapter 4 (this volume). Moving forward, however, it is important to keep in mind the potential limitations of relying solely on these resources. While these online summary resources are now available on a variety of topics, there are still many EBP questions for which there is no systematic review and no handy website or podcast to clearly lay out the research evidence. In other cases, sources may exist, but they may also be biased or limited in important ways. For example, states, funders, federal agencies, and nonprofits may all synthesize research evidence on interventions. States or funders may engage in this effort in order to makes choices about which programs to fund. Some of these reviews are very good; some of them are likely biased to serve a particular purpose or interest. Some organizations assemble research based on a systematic search of all available evidence, some invite intervention developers to submit research evidence supporting their work to be reviewed by an expert panel, and still others use experts to search for and assemble research findings. Relying on these other entities to identify and evaluate research evidence saves a whole lot of time. But, systematic reviews, registries, and clearinghouses are also limited in the topics they cover. So, if you are working in an area that is particularly new, or innovative, or a population for whom research is less available, you are less likely to find that research on these sites that may be directly applicable to your EBP question. Furthermore, if someone else summarizes the research for you, you won't be able to easily judge whether you think the research evidence included in the review is high quality or determine the degree to which the findings apply to your clients. In the end, it's a trade-off. If you do find yourself in a place where you need to conduct a search of the research evidence yourself, then you will want to become familiar with the services of a research librarian or refer to some of the tips provided in Chapter 4 (this volume).

Step 3: Critically Appraise the Evidence for Its Validity (Closeness to the Truth), Impact (Size of the Effect), and Applicability (Usefulness in Practice)

If you are looking at original research yourself and not relying on other entities to collect and assess the research for you, this step includes analysis of what you have in hand. When we talk about assessing validity of an intervention study, we're talking about how convincingly the authors make the case that the intervention is responsible for any of the outcomes that are achieved.

Most often in EBP we're interested in studies designed to establish the efficacy of a practice, intervention, policy, or program. We want to know how to best help our clients. There are lots of other practice questions of interest to social workers like "Which assessment tool is most effective at measuring suicide risk" and "What are the risk factors for developing Alzheimer's?" But, most often we want to know which intervention to use to get a particular outcome.

There are, of course, good intervention studies and crummy ones and everything in between. The key is to figure out which is which. Sadly, we can't offer you some sort of decoder ring or simple litmus test to tell the difference. No study is perfect, but being able to determine the strengths and weaknesses of any study is required if you're going to be able to smartly apply it, or choose not to apply it, to your work. Lots of textbooks are out there to help you do this kind of work, and we've made some suggestions in Appendix A. While not everyone is an expert in research methods and you may not be able to critically assess every detail of a sophisticated study, it does pay off to have some working knowledge of the characteristics of good studies, or at least what might be a red flag. This is, in part, why we teach basic research methods in social work programs—so that you can gain the general research knowledge necessary to assess the quality of studies. This is also why we think it makes a lot of sense for practitioners to get to know researchers working in their area with whom they might partner or consult on occasion. A researcher knowledgeable in an area of practice can quickly

---

Box 2.3

No study is perfect but being able to determine the strengths and weaknesses of any study is required if you're going to be able to smartly apply it, or choose not to apply it, to your work.

---

summarize the best available research evidence in a quick email or phone call, saving you a great deal of time and effort.

Typically, in this process of evaluating research, evidence priority is given to research findings described in published scientific studies; however, depending on the questions being asked other sources may be appropriate including internal evaluations or administrative data collected by your agency. Regardless of the source, the quality of the evidence and its limitations should be appraised using the most relevant and appropriate criteria. When critically appraising the research, it is necessary to assess not only the validity of the evidence but also the magnitude of the findings in terms of effect size. Effect sizes are one approach to determining how clinically or practically significant an intervention, policy, or program really is. Oftentimes, in social science research courses, such as those often taught in social work, we spend a lot of time talking about statistical significance. Statistical significance is a gauge of how likely the findings of the study were just a fluke—perhaps just due to chance. However, in some cases, interventions produce a statistically significant improvement in an outcome, but the improvement is so small as to be unimportant or not worth the resources needed to deliver it.

For example, imagine we have developed a new intervention called the "Bellamy Anxiety Destroyer" or BAD. We may try to convince you this intervention is highly valuable because we have research that shows our BAD intervention can statistically significantly reduce anxiety among professional social workers. Would you be interested? Maybe. Statistical significance is important, as that suggests that any improvements in anxiety that are observed in my study aren't likely due to chance. But, what if I said that, on average, my BAD intervention only reduces anxiety from a score of 95 to a score of 93 on a 100-point scale, where the higher you score on the scale the more anxiety you feel. What do you think of this intervention now?

We should be asking not only whether or not the outcomes are due to chance or not, but also "How impressive is the outcome?" and "How big is the impact compared to other interventions." This is precisely the type of information that effect sizes provide. Effect sizes are statistics, and there are actually several different ways that they can be calculated. These statistics are standardized. In other words, regardless of what you use to measure anxiety (client report on

---

Box 2.4

When critically appraising the research, it is necessary to assess not only the validity of the evidence but also the magnitude of the findings in terms of effect size.

---

a 100-point scale or some other measure) you can compare the magnitude of the impact across different studies. Table 2.1 provides some general guidelines in interpreting some of the most commonly used effect sizes, correlations, Cohen's *d* and odds ratios (Cohen, 1988; Miles & Shevlin, 2001). These are the approaches you're likely to run across when reading studies that examine social work relevant interventions.

So, for example, if there is an effect size of 0.1 or smaller using the correlation method, that is probably not even worth your attention. Most social science interventions achieve outcomes in the small to medium range. Small effects, those that range from 0.1 to 0.3 when using the correlation method may not be all that noteworthy either. Our BAD intervention would likely fall at this end of the spectrum. However, effect sizes shouldn't be interpreted in a vacuum. For example, if the outcome is very important, such as perhaps saving lives, a small effect may be very valuable. Say, for example, we could save one additional life just once every 1,000 times we used a new intervention as compared to the old intervention—that might be very valuable indeed. We also might be more interested in small effects if the outcome is very hard to improve at all or may have an impact on a large population. For example, there has been little research showing effective interventions for preventing child sexual abuse, so any program that could have an impact on that outcome at all might be very valuable—maybe even more so if that program could be widely applied across the United States and reduce the population rate of sexual abuse, even if only by a small amount.

In older studies, you may have a difficult time finding effect sizes reported in published manuscripts. They aren't actually that hard to calculate. If you find you need to do so, you can find a lot of free effect size calculators online, including

Table 2.1 **Interpreting the Magnitude of Effect Sizes**

Type of Effect Size	Small	Medium	Large
Correlation	0.10	0.30	0.50
Cohen's d	0.20	0.50	0.80
Odds Ratios	1.50	3.50	9.00

those on the Campbell Collaboration website. Usually all you need are means and standard deviations or percentage improvement across the intervention and control groups from study, and then you can plug that information into the online calculators to get your effect size. Happily, many journals now require researchers to specifically report effect sizes. But, for older studies, you may less often see them explicitly reported.

Finally, it's important to determine to what extent the evidence is applicable to their practice circumstances as well as the client's characteristics and needs. So, ask yourself, "Were the people in the study similar to your clients on key characteristics?" and "Was the context in which the intervention, policy, or program delivered similar to the one in which you are working?" For example, on balance there is less research on effective interventions for the very young, the very old, fathers, racial and ethnic minority groups, unmarried parents, and low-income populations, among others. Based on clinical theory and research evidence, we know that interventions may not work the same for all groups of people and in all contexts, so a mismatch between the best available research and the clients and contexts in which you practice could raise questions about the applicability of the findings to your work. Few studies are likely to be conducted with exactly the same community or clients you work with in exactly the same service context, but it's important to ask yourself how different the clients and contexts are between your practice and the research and critically consider how these differences may result in different outcomes should you apply the same intervention. Similarly, in macro level practice, just because some policy works well in Miami, Florida, does not mean that it will work as well in Philadelphia, Pennsylvania. Or, because a policy was effective in the 1980s, doesn't necessarily mean it will work well in the current sociopolitical context.

Step 4: Integrate the Critical Appraisal of the Research Evidence With Resources, Experience, and Client Characteristics, State, Needs, Values, and Preferences

In this fourth step of the EBP process the results of the evidence appraisal are integrated with what has been learned from prior practice experience, organizational and service system resources and constraints, and knowledge of the client's strengths, values, preferences, and circumstances. The role of the social worker at this stage is to integrate all of these different sources of evidence. For example, you may find a well-researched and effective intervention for treating anxiety among social workers that has a very nice effect size; however, you may also find that neither you nor your colleagues have been trained in the intervention, nor it is so prohibitively expensive it's not available anywhere in your community.

Box 2.5

When using the EBP process model, it is important to be transparent with clients about why you propose to provide a particular intervention to them, and any alternative options.

An important piece of this process is to communicate the best available research to clients along with these other considerations, so that your clients are as informed as possible about the intervention, policy, or program. This doesn't mean that you need to teach them about statistical significance and effect sizes but rather that you be able to translate this technical knowledge for them and answer questions they may have in a way that is understandable to them. When using the EBP process model, it is important to be transparent with clients about why you propose to provide a particular intervention to them, and any alternative options. Sometimes there are no real options, or no reasonable ones in any case. For example, service providers in rural areas may have only one mental health provider in the entire community, and there may be no feasible access to an alternative provider within a several hours drive. If that organization only provides cognitive-behavioral therapy (CBT), then that may be the only real option for treatment locally. Just so, from an EBP perspective, the providers should be able to articulate why they are providing a particular intervention to a particular client and what the research evidence indicates about using CBT for the problems for which their clients are seeking help.

This step may also require sharing what has been learned from professional colleagues' consultation or referral options outside of the provider or organization. All of this information should be shared with clients so that they will be empowered to make well-informed decisions regarding their participation in services. Not only does this practice align with informed consent; it also helps clients "buy-in" to the services. A client's belief that a service will be helpful to them is consistently related to better intervention outcomes (Asay & Lambert, 2008).

Step 5: Implement the Selected Intervention

We purposefully leave the description of this step brief. This step is really what the remainder of this book is about. Some depictions of the EBP process model don't even mention this step at all, as if the decision-making process described in Step 4 is enough to guide the way forward. Ha! If it was that simple, there would be no reason for this book. Successful implementation of any intervention or

Evidence-Based Practice Values

1. Client-centered practice

2. Transparency

3. Life-long learning

Figure 2.3 The three key values of the process model of evidence-based practice.

program really requires careful planning and preparation as well as ongoing monitoring.

Step 6: Evaluate the Effectiveness and Efficiency in Exercising Steps 1 to 5 and Seek Ways to Improve Upon Them Next Time

Social workers who use the EBP process model strive to keep up-to-date and seek to continuously improve their practice. An important element of this continuous improvement effort is the evaluation of each attempt to complete Steps 1 through 4. For example, research evidence is always evolving. New studies and interventions are being developed and tested all the time. Even established interventions are improved and retested. For example, one of us has developed an intervention designed to engage fathers in home visiting called Dads Matter-HV. After completing each of the two intervention studies on Dads Matter-HV, improvements and changes were made to the manual, training, and consultation process so that the intervention examined in the first study isn't the same one that is described in the current Dads Matter-HV manual.

You will likely need to re-engage in the steps of this process as you seek to update the interventions you are using, learn about new interventions, start a new program for your agency, or expand your practice to new clients or communities. This represents the third important value represented in the EBP process model: lifelong learning. There are always improvements to be made in practice and in the way we integrate research evidence into our practice decision making processes. Engagement in EBP requires constant reflection, critique, and course correction. Figure 2.3 lists the major values represented in the EBP process model.

In addition, we need to monitor how the practice, intervention, program, or policy is going for our clients, both as a group and at the individual level. Services need to be individualized, and we must recognize differences among clients. Even our best interventions don't work for everyone and all communities, and the most important client is the one in front of you. Interventions found to be effective in research studies may not have similar results with individual clients—there is always some variation. Accordingly, monitoring what happens when interventions are provided to individual clients is necessary so that adjustments can be made as necessary and alternative interventions can be implemented as needed.

It is also possible that over time an intervention does not work as well as it used to for many of your clients. Maybe the neighborhood is evolving with new immigrant or ethnic groups changing the linguistic and cultural needs of your clients. Maybe your clients are no longer interested in services provided in-person but are seeking similar services online. These changes in the groups of people you are working with or the culture and technology of the times can have an impact on how well your interventions work. These are just other examples of why it so important to continuously evaluate your practice and outcomes.

The EBP process model has a lot of utility and is well aligned with many values that are important to social work. However, it's not without challenges. Some of the most common challenges to this model of EBP come from misperceptions about EBP. Some of the most common misperceptions we have heard are that EBP is just a cost-cutting tool and that research dictates what is done to the detriment of other considerations such as clients' perspectives or practice experience. Neither of these, as we hope you can now see, is true. Research evidence is only one type of knowledge that is used in the process. Client and practitioner perspectives including pragmatic considerations are explicitly included. That being said, there are some very real challenges to using this model in social work practice, some of which are listed in Figure 2.4. As the field of social work advances along with technology, training, and research—we think these challenges will continue to be diminished over time.

While it is true that it may not be realistic for an individual practitioner to engage in all of the steps of the EBP process, it may be more manageable by a team of practitioners, which might also include researchers. Some of our research suggests that social work practitioners and researchers can feasibly and successfully work together to identify and apply the best available research using the EBP process model and that practitioners feel more confident and capable of

---

1. The steps of the EBP process take a great deal of time and resources.
2. Practitioners may not have the knowledge, training, or expertise needed to interpret research evidence.
3. The existing research evidence may be highly limited or ill reflect the people and contexts encountered in social work practice.

Figure 2.4 Evidence-based practice process challenges.

engaging in the process when they had researchers as team members (Bellamy, Bledsoe, Mullen, Fang, & Manuel, 2008). Another promising approach is to identify, appraise, consolidate, and translate research evidence for practitioners (essentially Steps 1–3 of the process) through a growing body of systematic reviews, registries, and clearinghouses.

Social worker training in EBP has also evolved a great deal in recent years. The use of research evidence in practice is explicitly described in both the National Associations of Social Workers' Code of Ethics and the 2015 Educational Policy and Accreditation Standards of the Council on Social Work Education, which guide the explicit and implicit curriculum of accredited social work programs in the United States. Increasingly social work programs provide training to students in the steps of the EBP process in addition to, or instead of, traditional research methods and statistics courses. Similarly, schools of social work are making efforts to support field supervisors, alumni, and others as they seek training on how to engage in EBP. There are many examples of training and supports for professionals in allied disciplines as well, including increasingly online training. One example of this is the Evidence-Based Behavioral Practice (EBBP.org) training portal, which is a partnership between professionals from the major health professions including social work designed to help practitioners learn and implement the EBP process model.

Finally, there is the challenge related to the limitations of the body of research that currently exists in terms of its fit with the clients and contexts of social work practice. There are a couple of promising trends that we think are likely to help fill in some of these gaps. First, increasingly, researchers are engaging in rigorous intervention research. While traditional intervention studies, or efficacy studies, are designed to test interventions under ideal circumstances, there is an increasing trend toward the production of intervention effectiveness research. Effectiveness studies are designed to test interventions under conditions that are more reflective of usual practice. For example, instead of engaging in research studies that employ practitioners that are specially hired, trained, and supervised directly by the researcher and carry out a study at a university hospital or clinic, researchers are increasingly partnering with providers who are already working in the field to test interventions with their usual staff and supervisors in community centers and clinics. In these studies, the eligibility criteria, or the rules that specify who can and cannot be in the study, are few and designed to better represent the clients that are seen day to day in the community. Another promising trend includes efforts to attend more carefully to cultural, racial, and ethnic minority groups, as well as other groups that have been historically poorly represented in research studies. For example, studies funded by the National Institutes of Health require that proposals be reviewed for the inclusion or exclusion of individual on the basis of sex, gender, race, ethnicity, and children to determine if the study is justified in including or excluding groups given the goals of the research and the methods proposed.

Discussion Questions

1. What different information is provided by tests of statistical significance and estimates of effect size?
2. What steps of the EBP process model seem most challenging? What can be done to address these challenges?
3. Why is it critical that social workers continuously evaluate their practice?

Evidence-Supported Interventions

In the last chapter we described the evidence-based practice (EBP) process model. While the EBP process was the original effort to bridge the research-practice gap, the definition of EBP quickly became obscured by a related effort to increase the rigor of research guiding practice by identifying these interventions for practitioners. In 1995, the American Psychological Association's Division 12 disseminated influential guidelines that identified whether an intervention should be considered to be evidence-based and a list of such interventions. Since this time, the American Psychological Association has clarified their definition of EBP as a decision-making process as described in the last two chapters and has since referred to what it once called evidence-based interventions as empirically supported treatments or interventions. Unfortunately, these conflated efforts led to some confusion about the definition of EBP, with many social workers understandingly adopting the *evidence-based practices* model of EBP (Parrish & Rubin, 2012; Rubin & Parrish, 2007). Since this time, we and many others within social work and other allied fields have tried to clarify the differences between these models. In this chapter, we describe what an empirically supported intervention is, how this idea has influenced the field, and what some of the strengths and limitations of this approach are.

Evidence-Supported Interventions

The use of evidence-supported interventions (ESIs) is arguably the most widespread approach to EBP—that is, if we consider any approach to bridging research knowledge and practice as EBP. The idea behind using ESI is that if practitioners use those interventions that are demonstrated as efficacious in research studies, rather than those that have been untested or perhaps even have been shown to do harm, then we are more likely to see good outcomes for clients in practice. If you use this approach, your task as a social work practitioner is to identify and use those interventions that have demonstrated efficacy or effectiveness through rigorous evaluations. One of the reasons that this approach is so popular is that it intuitively feels simple to refer to a list of interventions that work and use one of those. Certainly, this is easier than examining a pile of studies and sorting through the varied samples, methods, and outcomes. Digesting research is messy business. Funders also like using the ESI approach since they can just check whether providers are using their preferred interventions to support EBP. Just imagine how difficult it would be for a funder to determine whether each service provider you are supporting in your state used all six steps of the EBP process.

Lots of organizations, states, funders, and others have taken to this idea and run with it. For example, at the time of the writing of this book, the Families First Prevention Act recently authorized the creation of a new registry of interventions deemed to be evidence-based and approved for reimbursement for services provided to child welfare involved families. The State of Oregon legislature required that 75% of the funding for addictions and mental health services in the state go to fund ESI. The ESI identified by the state are listed on their website and have been approved by "independent review." Some entities, like Oregon, literally list approved ESI. Others will state evidence-based criteria, and service providers must defend how their programs and practices meet these criteria.

Evidence-Supported Intervention Criteria

There are some common criteria that are frequently used by policymakers, researchers, and other organizations who develop these lists of ESI. Generally, these criteria include the specific type of research design that can be used to establish whether an intervention works. This is most often a randomized controlled trial. But, sometimes well-designed and executed quasi-experimental trials are also accepted as very strong evidence, and therefore some lists include these types of studies when establishing their lists of ESI. When it comes to policy research, quasi-experimental, and other designs are much more common since randomization is not always a feasible approach to assessing policies. Usually, to be regarded as "evidence-based" or "evidence-supported," an intervention or program needs to demonstrate efficacy in more than one randomized controlled trial or quasi-experimental trial.

Sometimes additional criteria are specified in regards to how the intervention was tested and what the findings indicate. For example, to be considered an ESI criteria may specify that there is no evidence from studies indicating that the intervention does harm. Criteria also often include the requirement that studies use reliable and valid measurement approaches to assessing outcomes.

At least two randomized controlled trials have been conducted in usual practice settings that demonstrate the intervention produces positive outcomes.

Reliable and valid outcome measures have been used to establish positive outcomes The intervention does not cause risk or harm to clients.

The intervention has a manual or other documented specifications that describe the components of the intervention and how to provide it.

Access to training, technical assistance, or other supports to teach the skills of the intervention to those who wish to implement it.

Fidelity measures to ensure the intervention is implemented to a sufficient degree of quality.

Figure 3.1 Common criteria for establishing evidence supported interventions.

The reason is that if the measurement is questionable, then it's hard to trust the outcomes. In addition, criteria may require that studies be conducted in places that reflect the settings in which they are intended to be used. So, if the intervention is meant to be used in schools but was developed in clinics, that doesn't count. And, ideally the intervention should be tested against something, rather than nothing. This is called an "active" comparison group. That's because it's pretty easy to demonstrate your intervention is better than doing nothing. Even our BAD intervention probably does better than nothing.

Other criteria often used to establish whether an intervention is an ESI relate more to the supports that are available to implement the intervention with a high degree of quality and consistency in practice. To be designated as an ESI, an intervention should be *manualized*—or described with such a degree of specificity that you would know it when you saw it, you could measure whether it was being done correctly, and you could train others to do it correctly as well. Other rules might include the availability of training and the existence of fidelity measures. Fidelity measures are approaches to documenting that the intervention or program was done correctly, and we will go into much more detail on these in Chapter 9 (this volume). Figure 3.1 lists the common criteria used to determine whether an intervention should be considered evidence-supported.

Evidence-Supported Intervention Challenges

The use of ESI as your approach to EBP comes with some challenges. First, as we mentioned earlier, even our most effective interventions work for only a certain subgroup of people. Take cognitive-behavioral therapy (CBT), arguably one of the most prolific and well-researched interventions in mental health. In general,

CBT works for a lot of things that social workers commonly address like depression, anxiety, and aggression, for both children and adults and in groups and in individual practice. It's hard to think of a more flexible intervention model. Unfortunately, it doesn't work for everyone. Some folks just don't respond to CBT or respond to it very, very slowly. Or, some folks only partially respond to it and are left with symptoms or problems that still get in the way of their daily living. Other folks don't like it or give up on it before it can work. So, while CBT may be a good bet, it's not always going to work for everyone all the time. Or, it won't work for everyone to the degree we would like. So, it's a good thing to have options or alternative interventions to address these gaps.

Another challenge to using ESI as your approach to EBP is related to a challenge we already discussed around the process model of EBP: for many years, lots and lots of people that social workers serve were excluded from rigorous research studies. These groups include racial and ethnic minorities, children, older adults, folks living in rural parts of the country, and people with more than one problem or co-occurring disorders (e.g., depression and substance abuse). Now, researchers are getting better at addressing these issues as more underrepresented groups are being included in research. So, the tides are turning. But, the problem still remains that a lot of interventions were developed for, and deemed to be effective with, groups of people that don't reflect the diversity of folks that you likely work with in practice. So, things are getting better, but you still have to work with the client in front of you. You don't have the luxury of waiting for emerging research. An ESI might be shown to be effective using a very rigorous study, but if the study was conducted with only a small and select group of people, we don't actually know if it would work just as well with everyone else. Most important, we don't know if it will work with the client you are serving.

We'll give you an example here to illustrate. As a doctoral student, one of us was part of a research team that worked with a social service agency in New York City that was providing healthcare services to first- and second-generation Asian Americans. We formed a team at the agency as part of a research project in order to pilot an EBP process model approach (Bellamy, Bledsoe, Mullen, Fang, & Manuel, 2008). Together with agency staff and administrators, we searched for research that could guide their practice around mental health. So, this team

---

Box 3.1

An ESI might be shown to be effective using a very rigorous study, but if the study was conducted with only a small and select group of people, we don't actually know if it would work just as well with everyone else.

included both researchers and service providers. Those of us that were experts in research helped to search the available research evidence, appraise its quality, and summarize what we found in a way that was more understandable to the practitioners on our team. The practitioners on the team provided assessment information, details about the resources and needs of the clients and the agency, and other critical information. At the end of the project, we had a debriefing session where the participants could share their experiences participating in the process model. One of our favorite EBP quotes of all time came from this project. A social worker at the agency said that she thought that learning the EBP process was valuable but, at the end of the day, was really disappointed with the lack of research that included people who were like the people she worked with. She was amazed that the most rigorous study we could find was conducted, "with all white samples, like, in Minnesota?" If we are fortunate, this book will be widely read and used by lots of social workers, including those that work with white people in Minnesota (if that's you, send us an email, and I'll send you a copy of the study we found). The point is, the social worker we were collaborating with was not in Minnesota and couldn't find a single high-quality study that included large numbers of immigrant Asians in an urban U.S. community. So, she was more than a little frustrated and, frankly, suspicious of the findings described by the best available research study applied to her practice.

This is a very common experience. Oftentimes students and practitioners struggle when trying to find a study that is reflective of the clients and communities that they work with. Together we have come to learn that there are great big gaps in the research. It can be very difficult to find high-quality studies focused on topics of great interest to social workers like increasing healthcare access for undocumented workers, or alternative approaches to using restraints for youth in detention, or sexual health education approaches for Latino families. However, it's not just the sample of participants that you need to consider when deciding how much stock to invest in any given research study and its potential application to your work. There is also the context in which the study was conducted.

Lots of studies, particularly rigorous, highly controlled clinical trials testing the efficacy of interventions, are conducted under the best of circumstances that don't well reflect the realities of practice in the community. Participants are paid for their participation. Services are provided in hospitals, universities, or other well-resourced environments. Services are delivered by highly trained, relatively well paid, and well-supervised staff. Those services are monitored closely to ensure that they are maintained at a high quality. This, however, is not generally reflective of usual social work practice. Lots of social workers, including us, have worked in offices that are more likely a trailer behind a rickety old house, with two window unit air conditioners that didn't work very well in the Texas heat.

Some of us work without a supervisor, or don't get the luxury of regularly consulting with a supervisor. You may share that trailer with about five other people and a cat. And, after just two years on the job, you may be the most senior person in the trailer. Providing services on a shoestring budget and with staff that may or may not have a lot of supervisory support and a lot of turnover is qualitatively different than the conditions under which most highly controlled research studies are conducted. Do these things impact how well an intervention works? You bet.

This is all challenging whether you are using the EBP process model or ESI, and we are making progress in filling in some of these gaps as more studies are being conducted under real-world conditions. But, lots of them aren't. So, all this is to say that it's hard to determine whether an intervention works or doesn't work under any and all conditions. A lot of interventions work for some people and under some circumstances, but no intervention works for everyone under every circumstance. So, when we just produce lists of ESIs, we obscure all of this complexity, and you don't really know the degree to which the body of research anointing an intervention or program as evidence-based reflects the people and the places where you work. That, however, is not the only limitation of a strictly ESI approach to EBP.

We find that developing exclusive lists of interventions that "work" can stymie creativity and flexibility in practice. If states, or foundations, or other funders will only pay for those interventions that show up on a list, this ties the hands of practitioners who might otherwise develop creative new interventions that might work for different segments of the population. Many of these stakeholders are grappling with approaches to encouraging the use of ESI, while also introducing some flexibility into the process. You likely remember earlier we mentioned that the State of Oregon required 75% of services be evidence-based. That, at least, leaves 25% of services open for more creative, cutting-edge, or less well-researched approaches.

A strict abidance to only ESIs also causes other problems on the ground. We will tell you another story to illustrate. We have a friend and former colleague who did some work to educate judges about ESI for kids in child welfare. If you

---

Box 3.2

Lots of studies, particularly rigorous, highly controlled clinical trials testing the efficacy of interventions, are conducted under the best of circumstances that don't well reflect the realities of practice in the community.

know anything about child welfare services, you know that parent training is a keystone service in that system, and nearly every family served by child welfare gets some form of parent training. Parent training interventions are those that are designed to teach parents about child development and how to improve their parenting strategies to build better discipline, communication, and healthy routines for their families. However, most of the parent training classes provided in the field of child welfare are not evidence-based. Parents receive everything from highly sophisticated ESI like the Incredible Years model, to homegrown never-before-tested parenting classes, and everything else in between. According to our friend's story, after one judge participated in some training that highlighted this problem of inconsistent quality of services, the judge decided to correct the situation by court-ordering all of the parents in the courtroom to participate in evidence-supported parent training. This was definitely well intentioned and using court orders to improve services might be a plausible approach to improving the quality of services in some cases. However, in his particular jurisdiction, no evidence-supported parent training classes were offered within a hundred-mile radius of the courtroom. Even the most effective intervention won't do anyone any good if clients cannot get access to it.

Another problem is that many ESIs are not widely available in part because they are expensive and hard to maintain. Training, manuals, materials, and technical support can produce such a large bill for service providers that they opt not to uptake an intervention, or only partially uptake an intervention, or do not sustain the intervention with a high degree of quality. Training and technical support not only cost money, they also cost time. Time spent away from serving clients while participating in training is also time that service providers cannot bill for direct client services. And, because many social service agencies have such high turnover rate, it can be a very real concern for administrators to invest in expensive training for staff who aren't likely to remain at the agency for more than a year or two. Figure 3.2 outlines some common challenges to using ESI as an approach to EBP.

So, the ESI approach also comes with challenges. Despite these challenges, we don't want you to walk away from this chapter thinking that lists of ESI are not to be used. On the contrary, they can be really useful. For example, if you are new to a particular type of service, say because you are a student or you are starting a new job, looking over these lists can give you a quick sense of the gold standard interventions in the area. They may also give you information about which interventions are likely receiving the most support in your state or are favored by a particular funder. You can use them to make decisions about where you might want to invest time and money in training and other professional development efforts. ESIs are a great starting point. Depending on how the list was developed, how trustworthy you find the source, and how much information

Many interventions have only been tested with limited populations and service contexts, which may not reflect the clients, communities, or service contexts with which you are working.

The outcomes of studies are based on the average response to an intervention. Even the most effective interventions will not work for everyone.

Evidence supported interventions are expensive. Practitioners and agencies may not have the funding required to access training, manuals, consultation, and fidelity tools- particularly if multiple evidence supported interventions are needed.

Training, consultation, and other efforts needed to implement and sustain evidence supported interventions can be time consuming and take valuable staff time away from billable activities.

Some evidence supported interventions are rigid and not amenable to adaptations that may be needed do service delivery constraints, such as duration or dosage and format (e.g. group versus individual delivery, in-person versus online).

Figure 3.2 Common Challenges to Using Evidence Supported Interventions as an Approach to Evidence Based Practice.

they share about the process of developing the list, these lists of ESI can be very helpful indeed. But, in our opinion, selecting an intervention off of a list and using it in practice does not constitute the whole of EBP. We need a more varied and robust approach to the integration of the best available research evidence in social work practice.

Discussion Questions

1. What are some of the reasons that the use of ESI has been the most common approach to bridging research and practice?
2. What are some of the criteria that must be established for an intervention to be considered an ESI?
3. What are the strengths and weaknesses of each model of EBP (process model, ESI)?

4

Shopping for an
Evidence-Supported Intervention

We have spent the last few chapters learning about the evidence-based practice (EBP) process and identifying the distinction between this process and evidence-supported interventions (ESIs). Hopefully, by now, it is clear that the EBP process is the way in which practitioners make decisions about selecting the best ESI for their client or target population. This chapter builds upon the first three chapters by demonstrating how to "shop" for the best ESI using the EBP process, as well as how to engage in the evaluation of this ESI once selected. We want to emphasize that the implementation process of an ESI begins with identifying the most promising approach given its potential effectiveness and fit with the client or target population. The most comprehensive way to accomplish this—one that considers the best available research, the unique characteristics of your client population, and the fit with your agency—is to utilize the EBP process.

To illustrate this process and the importance of fit, let's consider the process of shopping for a personal automobile. Let's suppose you don't like trucks, have difficulty parallel parking with larger vehicles, need ample seating, and are so short you can't reach the pedals. Chances are you wouldn't want to be forced to purchase a truck. Most likely you'd want to find the automobile that's the right fit for you and, perhaps, your family. In addition to it having the right number of seats and features, you'd probably also want to make sure it gets good gas mileage and has positive reviews about its safety and durability from a valid and trustworthy source, right? In fact, we'd venture to suggest that many people spend a great deal of time considering not only whether the car is the right fit, but whether such a large investment is going to be worth the cost. The EBP process is much like this process—it requires consideration of the fit of the intervention for the target population or client and what you're able to provide, as well as critical thinking and consideration of valid research that informs whether the

---

Box 4.1

We want to re-emphasize that the success of such a process is contingent on a high quality of assessment of the client or target population.

---

intervention is effective enough to warrant the investment of resources for its implementation.

This EBP process is often referred to as "bottom–up" as the decision-making is made at the practitioner or programmatic level, as opposed to the "top–down" approach of being told which interventions an agency or program must use based on funding or other kinds of mandates (Gambrill, 2018). Imagine if you were told to just make that pickup truck work. You might be able to get around town, but it is clearly not the best option considering your preferences and needs. As social workers, the EBP process helps us to articulate our clients' needs from the ground level and advocate for services that are the very best fit based on the best available research, the client's preferences, and the agency context.

As noted in Chapter 1 (this volume), the EBP decision-making process integrates the best available research evidence with the client's characteristics and preferences, the practice context, and the practitioner's expertise. We want to re-emphasize that the success of such a process is contingent on a high quality of assessment of the client or target population. Such an assessment requires thorough information gathering, cultural sensitivity and humility, social work practice skills, and critical thinking to collaboratively identify the needs and preferences of this client/population (Parrish, Springer, & Franklin, 2015). This is Social Work 101. We want to start where the client is. It also requires clarity about intervention or program options based on cost, cost-effectiveness, and availability.

Shopping for an ESI

Crafting the EBP Question

The reason for a high-quality and thorough assessment is that you need to have a good sense of the presenting issue or issues, the kinds of outcomes you would like to accomplish, and the background characteristics of your client or target population when shopping for the best ESI. Once you have this background information, the next step is to develop a well-crafted and answerable EBP question. We briefly mentioned this in Chapter 2 (this volume), but here we lay out the specifics of how to construct such a question.

There are many acronyms out there to guide this process, such as PICO (patient, intervention, comparison intervention, and outcome), COPES (client-oriented, practical, evidence-search), and CIAO (client characteristics, intervention being considered, alternative intervention, if any, and outcome). PICO came out of evidence-based medicine; hence, the terminology focused on the patient. COPES was the acronym used in the first book written in social work on the EBP process (Gibbs, 2003), and the focus of this acronym was to emphasize that this process starts with a focus on what is of concern to the client and of practical importance to issues that arise in everyday practice. CIAO was the acronym developed and disseminated by Allen Rubin in *his Research Methods for Social Work* text, which can easily be remembered by thinking *ciao*, which means "hello" or "goodbye" (Rubin & Babbie, 2014). With this in mind, all of the components of a well-developed EBP question have the same main parts.

There are four main components that may be a part of your EBP effectiveness question. To be consistent with other allied fields who may engage in this process, we'll stick with the PICO format. All PICO questions are framed, obviously, as a question.

1. *Patient/client and problem*: This part of the question describes the client or target population, the context and presenting problem. This involves considering things such as the age, culture/ethnicity, gender, delivery setting, and issue being addressed (e.g., domestic violence, caregivers of Alzheimer's, teen pregnancy). The reason for being specific with this description is that these descriptors will help in the search for the best available evidence that fits best for your client or target population.

2. *Intervention (what you might do)*: If you have a sense of the existing evidence base for the issue you are addressing, you might already have an intervention in mind. In this case, you would list the intervention in your question. For example, you may know that trauma-focused cognitive behavioral therapy (CBT) tends to work well in addressing trauma symptoms among adults, but we may not know if that is the best approach for the target population we are working with.

3. *Comparison intervention if relevant (alternative course of action)*: If you have a general sense of the literature base and know there are really two primary intervention options that you are examining, then including this comparison intervention may be relevant and important to your practice question and subsequent literature search. Following up on the prior example, you may know that trauma-focused CBT and EMDR (eye movement sensitization reprocessing) are both well-supported in the literature, among many other trauma interventions. So, your EBP effectiveness question may focus

on answering which of the two interventions is the best fit for your client or target population.

4. *Outcomes (what you want to accomplish)*: This part of the question includes the key outcomes you hope to accomplish in your work with the client or target population. This should be based on the goals identified in your assessment.

One approach to putting the EBP effectiveness question together is to develop a table such as the one illustrated in Figure 4.1 where the key elements are populated (Gibbs, 2003). If the column doesn't apply, then it can be skipped. Generally, the one that gets most often skipped is the comparison column. Sometimes you just want to know if a particular intervention gets the outcomes you want for clients like yours, and you don't want to limit it to two interventions unless you are very familiar with the intervention options to start with.

What is the most effective teen pregnancy and HIV/ sexually transmitted infection (STI) risk reduction intervention for female adolescents (primarily African American) receiving services in the juvenile justice system? If we were to know the interventions in advance that we were looking at, our question may look something like this: If female adolescents (primarily African American) receiving services in the juvenile justice system are given the Imara intervention (DiClemente et al., 2014) or Sisters Saving Sisters, which will result in reduced risk of pregnancy, HIV, and STIs? Why is this level of specificity in our questions important? It's important because it allows us to extract several potential search terms that will inform our search of the relevant literature to answer this practice question. For example, in our first question we can extract terms such as "teen pregnancy," "HIV," "STI," "female," "adolescent," "African American," and "juvenile justice." This provides us with a much better start when searching for relevant teen and sexual health programs than just looking for teen pregnancy prevention programs more broadly. In addition, as we'll see in the next section, we can use these terms to identify synonyms that help us to expand our search

P: Client/Target Population Type, Characteristics and/ or Problem	I: Intervention Option One (if known)	C: Comparison Intervention (if known)	O: Desired Outcomes
Female, juvenile justice, adolescent, largely African American	Not Known (looking for the best available intervention)	Not Known (looking for best available intervention)	Reduction of risk of pregnancy, HIV, and STIs

Figure 4.1 Example PICO question.

to ensure we are including all aspects of the literature. For example, the term "adolescent" has synonyms such as "teen" and "youth" that may be helpful for a search.

There are some very important considerations when posing an effectiveness EBP question. First, a question should not be posed with the goal of finding evidence to support the answer one is looking for. Another important value represented in the EBP process is to always be open to conflicting evidence and to account for it when making decisions and to be honest brokers of knowledge and transparent about what the field says with our clients. We need to recognize our tendency to confirm what we know and be consciously open to what may not. Second, as previously noted, questions need to be specific enough that they yield a useful answer for guiding practice. If our question is specific and well-posed, it will save time and the relevant literature can be more quickly identified. Finally, not all EBP questions are effectiveness questions.

The authors of this model emphasized that there will be many instances in which practitioners will need additional information before they can truly understand a client or target population they are working with. These are called "background questions," and they can relate to issues such as more accurate assessment (which screening instrument works best?), how to modify risk factors or enhance protective factors, how to better understand a particular client population (perhaps through qualitative research), and other kinds of questions that inform practice. This is why many proponents of the EBP approach emphasize that the EBP process does not just concern itself with evidence from randomized controlled trials (RCTs). For more information on how to construct such EBP questions, we recommend that readers consult the original sources—*Evidence-Based Medicine: How to Practice and Teach EBM* (Straus et al., 2011), *Evidence-Based Practice for the Helping Professions* (Gibbs, 2003), or *Critical Thinking and the Process of Evidence-Based Practice* (Gambrill, 2018).

Once you've composed an answerable EBP practice question, you're ready for the next step!

Seeking Out the Best Available Research

The next step—step 2 of the process—is to search for the best available evidence to answer your EBP question. As mentioned earlier, one of the reasons for developing a specific and answerable EBP question is to generate useful terms to guide the search process, especially if you are utilizing large databases. However, the next question is where you should start your search for the best available evidence. It can feel overwhelming thinking about where to start, especially since anyone can create a web page these days and make claims about effective practice approaches. However, if you become familiar with some of the legitimate

---

Box 4.2

One of the reasons for developing a specific and answerable EBP question is to generate useful terms to guide the search process, especially if you are using large databases.

---

online sources and how they work, it can save you time and reduce concerns that you may be consuming sites that lack credibility or may be biased.

Online Meta-Analyses and Systematic Reviews

If you want to save time, the best thing to do is to start by looking for credible meta-analyses or systematic reviews that synthesize the literature on specific practice-related questions that align with your EBP question. How do you know if they are credible? Well, ideally the study is not being done by the developers of the intervention or program, as they may have a vested interest in finding a certain kind of result. As noted in Chapter 2 (this volume), two of the most credible sources of systematic reviews are the Cochrane and Campbell Collaborations, as they have rigorous processes in place to reduce the impact of bias. While a copy of the full Cochrane review—which focuses more on medicine and mental health practice questions—requires purchase, the summary is free for download. Perusing this summary may help you to determine if it is worth the purchase or the effort to reach out to someone with access at a university to see if they can get a copy for you. Also, as mentioned in Chapter 2, they have the handy recorded podcast summaries you can listen to that can help you stay up to date on the literature while cleaning your house, walking your dog, or sitting in traffic. What an efficient EBP practitioner you will be! In contrast, all of the reviews on the Campbell Collaboration website, which focus more on social interventions (e.g., education, child welfare, criminal justice) are free. The Campbell Collaboration does not yet have podcasts, but we hope they will soon.

Online Databases

While in school, you have access to a rich collection of databases through your university library. We encourage you to take full advantage of this while you can. Nurture and develop the evidence-based practitioner in you and search the evidence to your heart's delight. Once you graduate and lose your library privileges, do not despair. There are still ways to stay connected to online databases. Our first recommendation is to go and get a library account at

> *Box 4.3*
>
> Once you have set up a public library account, one of the best things you can do is partner up with a research or reference librarian there to see if they can help you navigate available databases and learn options for getting access to materials that are unavailable by using interlibrary loan.

your public library, if you have not already. Once you have that information, you should be able to log in and view the online databases that your local library has purchased. For example, while we are both professors and have access to our university libraries, one of us checked our online library account and found that this local public library also offers EBSCO Academic Search Complete, PubMed Central, and Medline Plus. On top of this, the public librarian shared that public libraries in Texas offer something called the TexShare card, which allows a public library member with this card to access 68 shared Texas university and public library databases in one place online (but you have to ask, and very few people get them). Voila! Access to several journals in our field that are typically not open access at the touch of our fingers. Once you have set up a public library account, one of the best things you can do is partner up with a research or reference librarian there to see if they can help you navigate available databases and learn options for getting access to materials that are unavailable by using interlibrary loan. Librarians have a great deal of training in how to efficiently navigate search engines and get access to research articles, books, and reports. Local public librarians are often very happy to help you use their online databases. Very few people typically ask.

If you do not live in Texas and your public library options are less than perfect, consider befriending a local academic. They may be able to access the resource for you. Moreover, if you serve as a field instructor or adjunct at a university, you may also have opportunities for your own access to the university library if you request it. Many universities are now providing this kind of access. We have also found that if all else fails, simply emailing the author of the study and requesting a copy of the article can work too.

Other Online Sources: Google Scholar, Registries, and Clearinghouses

The problem with starting with databases at a local public library, unless they are quite comprehensive, is that you may miss out on some important studies that are not indexed in that database. This is one of the reasons we like Google

Scholar. Please make special note that this is *Google Scholar*, not *Google*. Google will pull up all kinds of things, both scholarly and not scholarly, and you truly have to wade through the weeds to find the flowers. Google Scholar, on the other hand, is focused on the published, peer-reviewed literature. The nice thing about Google Scholar is that it catches everything that is published online, so you don't run into the problem of missing important studies that are not indexed in a database. For this reason, many times we start our search here to see what is available and what is open access. Quite a bit of research is available online for free public download. All research that is federally funded is required to be available for public consumption. This is your tax dollars at work. It has also become quite common for authors of research to put their last submitted draft of a manuscript online prior to printing for public consumption, depending on the policies of the journal they are publishing in. These often pop up as available on ResearchGate. So, you actually have much better luck in getting access to research online now than ever, and we suspect this will get better as there is a paradigm shift towards providing the public with open access to research.

Depending on your EBP question and how much research evidence exists to answer the question in Google Scholar, you may find a million gazillion trillion references. OK, that may be exaggerating, but still, it might be a lot. If you are feeling overwhelmed and you have not already looked for a systematic review or meta-analysis, now would be the time to check Campbell and Cochrane Collaborations to be sure it has not been done. If you don't find one here, it does not mean it has not been done. You can search more broadly by entering the terms "systematic review" or "meta-analysis" into Google Scholar with your other key search terms and see what you find. Another option is to visit relevant online registries or clearinghouses. Some examples of these registries are provided in Figure 4.2.

While the downside of these online resources (registries and clearinghouses) is the lag time to reviewing and disseminating the most recent research, if there is a lot of research that has been done, they are a great place to see what is recommended based on the reviews of methodological experts. These methodological experts traditionally review the studies using a set standard of methodological rigor for various intervention approaches. In addition to getting their evidence ratings, they often provide information on available training manuals, the cost of the intervention, and other considerations for adoption and implementation of the approach. So, one way to approach this search would be to review these relevant online resources, while also looking for only the most recent information in Google Scholar that may not yet be reflected on these sites. Who knows, you may find the perfect intervention that fits like a glove for your client or target population that is hot off the press. Ideally, an intervention would have been replicated in more than one RCT, but if it is an intervention that has shown

1. Office of Juvenile Justice and Delinquency Prevention's Model Programs Guide: http://www.ojjdp.gov/mpg

2. The California Evidence-Based Clearinghouse for Child Welfare: https://www.cebc4cw.org

3. Evidence-Based Practices for Substance Use Disorders: http://lib.adai.washington.edu/epbsearch.htm

4. The Evaluation Center's EBP Metabase: http://libr.adai.washington.edu/ebpsearch.htm

5. National Cancer Institute Research Tested Intervention Programs: http://rtips.cancer.gov/rtips/index.do

6. National Institute on Drug Abuse Examples of Research Based Drug Abuse Prevention Programs: https://www.drugabuse.gov/publications/preventing-drug-abuse-among-children-adolescents-in-brief/chapter-4- examples-research-based-drug-abuse-prevention-programs

7. Social Programs That Work: https://evidencebasedprograms.org

8. PubMed: https://www.ncbi.nlm.nih.gov/pubmed/

Figure 4.2 Registries and clearinghouses.

efficacy more broadly with this or other populations, this would suggest strong promise.

Now that we have discussed the most efficient sources for searching for the best research evidence, let's explore how to be even more efficient when searching within databases or Google Scholar. Being a smart EBP shopper means being a savvy shopper—one who does not waste too much time sifting through or reading irrelevant articles. As a busy practitioner, who has time for that?

Searching Strategies in Databases and Google Scholar

So back to the EBP question. The first step in efficient searching is to use those key search terms that you identified in your question. Going back to our previous example, our question was, *What is the most effective teen pregnancy and HIV/STI risk reduction intervention for female adolescents (primarily African American) receiving services in the juvenile justice system?* From this question, we were able to extract the following search terms: "teen pregnancy," "HIV," "STI," "female," "adolescent," "African American," and "juvenile justice." We were able to use these terms to identify synonyms that help us to expand our search to ensure that we would catch every iteration of each term in the literature. For example, the term "adolescent" has synonyms such as "teen" and "youth" that may be helpful for a search. What other synonyms can you come up with? Perhaps "sexually transmitted diseases" for STI (sexually transmitted infection), or "Black" for African American, or "criminal justice" for juvenile justice? The key is to develop a list of synonyms and use these terms for your search.

The next step is to use some handy-dandy search tricks including truncation, wildcards, and Boolean logic. Truncation helps you to search all variations on the root of a word without writing out each word separately. So, for example, if you are interested in research focused on children, you can enter "child*" and this will search all words with the same root including: child, children, children's, and childhood. Wildcard logic substitutes a symbol for one letter of a word, essentially allowing the database to look for all variations of spelling with regard to that letter. For example, using "wom!n" will yield woman and women. Boolean logic can also be very helpful when searching. This logic utilizes the terms "and," "or," or "not." When you use the term "and," it your search will look for both terms together, so it narrows your search to only results that include all of the terms connected by "and." If you use the term "or" your search will be broadened to look for both terms by essentially telling the database that any of these terms can be present to include a result. This is best when you're looking for synonyms, such as "youth" and "adolescent" and "teenager." It's important if you use "or" to remember to put your search terms in parentheses so that they are not confused with the rest of your search term. "Not" is a Boolean operator used to exclude certain terms that you do not want to include in your search. Finally, full phrases that are not single words should be put in quotation marks. So, as an example, when searching for evidence to answer the above EBP question, we might try the following search term:

> "Teen pregnancy" and HIV and [STI or "sexually transmitted infections" or STD or "sexually transmitted diseases"] and female and [adolescent or youth or teen] and [Black or African American] and intervention and [effective or RCT or quasi-experimental design or meta-analysis or systematic review]

Notice we added some terms at the end that correspond with the kinds of studies that might help us to know if an intervention is effective. In this case, since we've asked an effectiveness EBP question, the studies we are most interested in including RCTs, quasi-experimental designs, meta-analyses or systematic reviews. Looking at this term and its logic, do you think there could be any limitations or problems? Specifically, do you think that it could be too limiting? What would you do if nothing comes up? Or if too much comes up? If nothing comes up, it may be that research has not been done in this area with this population (although in this case, we know it has). If this is the case, as you do your own EBP search, you will need to take some of the more specific terms away and go wider or perhaps take the "and" Boolean operator out of your search term. This is an iterative process that takes some patience and creativity. You can't just enter in one set of search terms and know the breadth or limitations of the evidence.

It is the same situation if you get too much. In that case you may have to limit the search and try iterations where you take out terms, selecting the best terms connected with the "and" operator. For example, you might take out the term "effective" if you get a lot of reviews of studies that look at the evidence base, but that do not report on original research or a true statistical synthesis of the research. As you practice this process, it will get easier, and you will get a better sense of the evidence available for the area of practice you're interested in and that relates to your client. The upside is that once you've done this and you're pretty familiar with what's there, you won't have to search as deeply the next time. You can primarily focus on the new stuff. How's that for being a savvy EBP practitioner?

A final consideration to keep in mind is that you may enter your search terms differently depending on the database, however the logic will remain the same. Some will want you to enter the entire search term, as previously shown, while others will provide rows where you have a drop-down option to select "and" or "or" or "not," and you will simply need to enter your terms in the right row. As such, it's important to take a few moments to become familiar with the database you are using and read over any user guides. For example, if you're using PubMed, there is a great tool that helps you find synonyms within the database to search for articles called MeSH (Medical Subject Headings) terms. It also helps you to identify vocabulary words or synonyms that perhaps had not yet been considered that are associated with your area of interest, as well as subheadings or quantifiers to look at subgroupings of the literature. Online search engines are getting increasingly sophisticated and offer more and more of these types of tools.

Now that you've looked and narrowed down your sources of evidence—which could have been from a variety of online databases, clearing houses, Google Scholar, etc.—it's time to sit down and critique it for its validity and applicability. We're on to step 3!

Appraising the Evidence for Effectiveness

At step 3, we may have found primarily articles, a great systematic review or a program or two on a clearing house website. Regardless of what you found, it is time to put on our critical thinking, research appraisal hats to see whether the evidence for an intervention or program supports its adoption. This is the step where many practitioners decide it is time to check out. Why can't the experts just do this for us? We don't have time. We believe it—there isn't much time in practice. We've both been there. However, this part of the process can be very fun and meaningful, and it is not quite as difficult as it seems. In fact, if you engage others it goes quickly and it's more fun, so perhaps develop a team of likeminded practitioners or administrators who will join you and share the fruits of this labor? Revisiting the shopping analogy here, savvy friends that share information about the best products and deals save lots of time and money. If you don't have likeminded friends, don't worry. It's most likely you will work with the same kinds of clients and issues if you stay in the same agency or focus your practice in a particular area. After you invest the time once, it won't take nearly as long to stay up on the literature in the future.

But, you ask, it's not as difficult as it seems? No, it is not. You don't have to know and understand every kind of statistical analysis or every special research design feature to critically appraise research. Since we are looking at EBP in the context of shopping for an ESI, we would be looking for the best available research evidence to support the efficacy or effectiveness of an intervention. The key things you need to understand are different group design features (random assignment, control group) that improve the internal validity of a design, ways to reduce measurement bias, how to interpret the results (statistical significance, effect size and substantive significance), and how to assess the external validity of the study. Sound overwhelming? We promise it will get easier as we work through what to look for in the following discussion. There are several useful tools, called evidentiary checklists (provided in Appendix B), that may be useful when you are reviewing research studies. They can be very useful for comparing and contrasting studies and keeping a nice record of what you've found.

Figure 4.3 shows the research hierarchy for intervention questions. There are three things that must be achieved to claim cause and effect—in this case, we're talking about the intervention causing the outcomes. This is called establishing a causal relationship. These three things include (a) time order, (b) correlation, and (c) ruling out alternative explanations for the change in the outcome variable. The first, when it comes to outcome studies, is usually achieved. This simply means the intervention must precede the change in the outcome variable. When looking at Figure 4.1, this occurs for all kinds of studies with the exception of correlational studies listed at Level 6 and other approaches listed in Level 7. Correlational studies are typically cross-sectional (measured at one point in time). With regard to correlation, this simply means that the variables being studies are statistically related to one another—or that change in intervention is associated with change in the outcome.

The most difficult aspect of causality to establish is the third requirement, ruling out alternative explanations for the change in the outcome variable. This is where the fun and critical thinking comes in. These tricky alternative

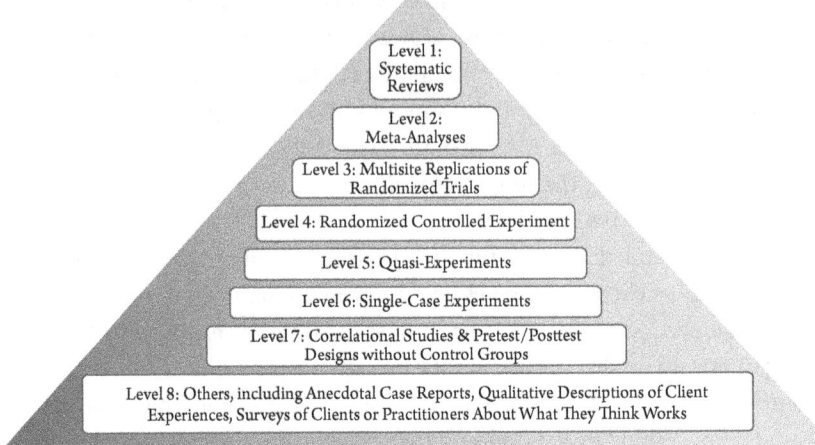

Figure 4.3 Research hierarchy for intervention studies. *Source:* Adapted from Rubin & Bellamy, 2012.

explanations for changes in the outcome variable are called *threats to internal validity*. Ideally, we want to use designs with high levels of internal validity to guide our practice, and this requires design features that help rule out common threats to internal validity such as history, maturation or the passage of time, regression to the mean, testing, differential attrition, and a selection bias. If this sounds like another language, stay with us, it's really not as difficult as it sounds. There are just a few key design features that help us control for these threats.

The key design features that distinguish each of these designs are the presence of—drum roll please—a control group, random assignment, and replication. Yep, just three things. At the top of the hierarchy are systematic reviews and meta-analyses, each of which statistically or otherwise synthesize research from multiple intervention studies on specified outcomes. We lead with systematic reviews as higher on the research hierarchy than meta-analyses simply because the systematic review process—how articles are located, included, and appraised—must be very specific so that other researchers could easily replicate it and they use strategies to reduce bias. A similarity between them is that they both often use fancy, advanced statistical methods to synthesize the research of available studies. On the next two steps are RCTs, with Level 2 encompassing RCTs that have been replicated at least one time or that are multisite RCTs. The value of a multisite RCT from an evidentiary standpoint is its enhanced external validity given implementation in more than one context. In other words, we get more confident in the intervention's ability to achieve change when it works in more than one place with different clients and communities. Level 3, in contrast, includes at least one well-designed RCT. RCTs randomize individuals or sites to an intervention condition. This randomization, when the sample size is large enough, helps to equalize the groups to ensure that they are comparable. Everyone has an equal chance of being in each condition, and over time, with enough in each group, any differences between the groups (e.g., gender, age, scores on outcome variables) even out. In research speak, when we have comparable groups through random assignment, we have alleviated a selection bias.

Threats to Internal Validity

Selection bias is when one group in a study has different outcomes because of something other than the intervention, which could include being more motivated than the other group, having worse scores on the outcome variable of interest to start, or having an overrepresentation of a characteristic in one group that makes this group more amenable to change. For example, let's suppose we have developed a fitness intervention. We let folks sign up for the condition they would like—a combined fitness intervention (combined exercise and nutrition) or exercise alone. All of the younger folks who want to continue to eat what they want to sign up for the exercise alone condition, and the older folks (who are struggling with the middle-aged bulge) sign up for the combined fitness intervention. At the end of the study, there is no difference between the two groups; they both lost the same amount of weight. Would you conclude the weight loss intervention did not work? Or might the fact that there is no difference between the groups be that younger individuals, who all signed up for the exercise alone group, had an easier time getting fit because of their age? In other words, for the younger ones, adding exercise alone yielded the same improvements in fitness as middle-aged adults improving both nutrition and exercise. The problem with a selection bias is that both explanations—that age impacted the outcomes and that the intervention are not effective—are both completely plausible. A better experiment would use *random assignment*, not self-selection, to the groups so that both groups have the same age on average. With this (and other variables) controlled, we can attribute the outcome to the intervention and not the differences between the groups.

Randomization assumes we have more than one group. To know if an intervention is effective, we need to compare a group that gets this intervention with a group that doesn't. The group that doesn't get the intervention is called a *control group*. Why do we need a control group? We need a control group to rule out other potential explanations for why the intervention group may have gotten better or improved. These potential explanations are history (events that happened during the study), maturation or passage of time, and statistical regression to the mean. For those of you who were social science undergraduate majors, you may be having flashbacks to your research methods class. Try to hang in there with us; it really isn't that difficult to understand. Let's start with the concept of *history*. The first thing to understand is that this does not have to do with what happened in the past—sometimes folks get confused by the term. It has all to do with contemporaneous events or what happens during the course of the delivery of an intervention that could have been responsible for the change in the outcome variable. For example, if an intervention is being tested that targets smoking cessation in teens across the state of Texas, and during the study, a tobacco tax makes the costs of cigarettes twice the cost, this cost and not the smoking cessation intervention may be the reason teen smoking goes down. The cost would be considered a contemporaneous event or history. Now, let's say that instead of having just one group, we had a group of teens that were randomized to the smoking cessation group and a treatment as usual condition that provided information about the health effects of smoking. Further, let's say that despite the increase in the tobacco tax, the smoking cessation group significantly reduced smoking compared to the information only group. Having this control group allows us to rule out history or contemporaneous events as both groups were exposed to the change in the tobacco tax.

Now, let's move to the concept of *maturation or passage of time*. Let's say that we designed an intervention to treat trauma symptoms and reduce the chances that individuals develop posttraumatic stress disorder (PTSD) following major disasters such as hurricanes or wildfires. The intervention is designed to provide support through case management and individual counseling. If you only had the intervention group and no control group, it would be hard to know if individuals would simply cope better on their own over time (hence the reason it is called passage of time). There are a lot of things, like grief and loss, for example, that generally get better with time with little or no intervention at all. However, if you randomly assign half the people in a study to a grief and loss intervention group and the other half to a control group that doesn't get the treatment, the same opportunity for improvement over time is possible for both groups. If the intervention group has much more improvement than those receiving the traditional intervention, then that would provide support for the intervention by ruling out the possibility of both history and passage of time. Maturation differs from passage of time in that it has to do with improvement due to growing or developing. This can be illustrated in an example of a substance abuse prevention program for young adults on a college campus. If evaluated without a control group, it would be difficult to know if these young adults simply matured or grew out of risky behaviors that are more common during adolescence. However, with a control group, both groups are equally as likely to mature or grow out of typical substance abuse behavior, and you guessed it, if the intervention group does better than the control group, it would provide support for the intervention and rule out history and maturation.

Quasi-Experimental Designs

Next on the hierarchy are quasi-experimental designs. "Quasi" means they are not quite experimental because they lack random assignment. However, they have design features that attempt to make the groups comparable without random assignment. Like RCTs, this design requires at least two groups. But we typically call the group that doesn't get the intervention a comparison group instead of a control group. These features may include matching on key characteristics or scores on an outcome variable. The downside, however, is that even with all of this effort to make the groups comparable, there could be an unmeasured factor that the groups were not matched on that explains why one group did better or worse than the other. In other words, you really cannot rule out selection bias. As an evidence-based practitioner, you have to critically analyze the case the researcher has made for the comparability of the groups. Have they provided evidence on key background characteristics and the outcome variable that the two groups are similar statistically at baseline? What important variables may not have been reported on that may make the groups different? How were the two groups selected? Could one group be more motivated than the other to start? These are all key questions to ask when looking at this particular design.

Single-System Designs

As we step down, we come to single-system designs. These are designs that have a sample size of one, so they are not highly *generalizable*, which is why they are lower on the evidentiary list. Generalizable is the degree to which the findings of a study could be applied more broadly. With larger samples with more diversity and or with replication across a lot of diverse samples, we increase the generalizability of findings. Single-system designs have neither large samples nor replication across a lot of diverse samples. However, some of these designs have high levels of internal validity given design features that track the outcome variable at regularly spaced intervals (daily, weekly, etc.) where the intervention is alternatively withheld and provided. When the intervention is provided, ideally you expect to see improvements in the outcome, and then when it is withheld, those improvements decrease. This design gets used more often in certain areas like education where simple and concrete interventions like schedule changes, seating arrangements, or co-teachers can be easily provided and removed to observe improvements in things that can change rapidly like classroom behavior. High-quality single-system designs also have the key feature of multiple baselines. Multiple baselines are multiple periods where the intervention is and is not provided and replication can be demonstrated across an individual, settings, individuals, or behaviors. Generally, these studies present a graph demonstrating the relationship between improvement in outcomes and the timing of the intervention period. Since these designs are low on generalizability, you want to be cautious using them to guide your practice. Some practitioners use these designs to evaluate their practice since they can be easily used with an individual, group, or family. You may find this design to be a useful approach for evaluating your practice.

Pre-Experimental Designs

Below single-subject designs on the hierarchy, we see pre-experimental designs. These are not ideal because they don't do a good job controlling for other explanations for improvements in outcomes. However, if this is all you have got in terms of research evidence, it may be better than nothing. In this case, you have to take this information in the context of its limitations and perhaps lean more heavily on other theoretical sources of knowledge and established practice wisdom. It is important to realize that if you have searched for the evidence, and it is not there, you've got to use the best-established evidence there is. This still makes you an EBP practitioner, because at least you engaged in an honest search for the very best available research.

Measurement of the Outcome Variable

There are a few more important aspects to critiquing intervention research. A study with the very best and most flawless design can still be flawed if the measurement of the outcome variable was biased or not measured well or if the measures are not truly meaningful. It's important that the author of the study provide adequate support for the reliability and validity of their outcome measures. Reliability has to do with the consistency of the measure across items in a scale measuring the same construct (internal consistency reliability), across individuals rating behavior or other phenomena (interrater reliability), or over time (test–retest reliability). Reliability is measured using a scale of zero (no reliability) to 1.0 (perfect reliability). What you want to look at, when an author is reporting on the reliability of a measure is how close to 1.0 it is. If it is under 0.70, particularly if there are many items in the scale, it's not a very reliable measure. Good is generally considered 0.80 or above, and excellent is 0.90 or above.

The validity of a measure has to do with whether it is measuring what it is intending to measure, and to what degree of accuracy. A measure must be reliable for it to be a valid measure. There is a hierarchy of validity that a researcher typically progresses to establishing when they develop a new scale or measure. First, it must have *face validity*, which just means that the items in the scale make sense in describing the construct of interest. For example, if the researcher is planning to measure anxiety, the items should be consistent with this by including items that may say, for example, "I worry about things that are out of my control." It makes sense, on the face of it, that that kind of item would describe anxiety. The next level of validity is *content validity*, and that is when experts in the field of the construct being measured agree that the items on the scale or in a measurement questionnaire cover the construct or subject matter measured. Next, there is *criterion validity*, and that is the degree to which a measurement instrument is associated with an external criterion in the way it is theorized to. This can take many forms—known groups validity, concurrent validity, or predictive validity. With *known groups*, you're taking a group that you know has a particular trait that you're trying to measure—say, anxiety with a group you know had received a clinical diagnosis of anxiety. Then you're going to get a second group of individuals who you know have not been diagnosed with anxiety and do not have concerns with anxiety symptoms. You would give your new anxiety scale to both groups and see if the anxious group scores significantly higher. They should, right? This would establish known groups validity. Other kinds of criterion validity include *predictive validity* and *concurrent validity*—one of which shows an association of your measure of anxiety with a future event (e.g., diagnosis with an anxiety disorder, missed days at work, or illness) and the other that simply shows an association of your measure with other similar and well established measures (such as the Beck Anxiety Inventory).

Finally, there is *construct validity*. This can be established for a measurement scale by testing *factorial validity*, which is a fancy term for statistical analyses that assess whether the items in a scale measure the same number of proposed scales or subscales. For example, the factorial validity has been supported for the Multidimensional Anxiety Scale for Children, second edition, to measure not just anxiety, but five kinds of anxiety, obsessions and compulsions, and physical symptoms related to panic and tenseness. We know that we can depend on all of the various subscales because the developers of the scale conducted a factorial analysis and the items for each subscale "held together" and did not load on other dimensions. In contrast, if you have one scale measuring one construct, factorial validity would mean that all of the items held together or "loaded" onto one construct. Another way to demonstrate construct validity is to demonstrate *both* convergent and discriminant validity. Why do we italicize *both*? Because you cannot establish construct validity without both. Got it? Good. So why is this? It's because with validity we are concerned with accuracy—specifically that we are measuring precisely what we are intending to measure, and not some closely related, but different construct. So how does this work exactly? The researcher proposes a study where they collect data from a large sample of individuals where they administer their new amazing short 10-item scale that measures clinical depression along with the Beck Depression Inventory (which also measures clinical depression using 21 items) and the Generalized Anxiety Scale 7-item scale and the 10-item Rosenberg Self-Esteem Scale. So, the research participants fill out all these scales—a total of 48 items. When they're done, you calculate the scale scores and see if they are related to each other. The goal is that your new 10-item depression scale would correlate more highly with the Beck Depression Inventory (which also measures clinical depression) than the Generalized Anxiety Scale and the Rosenberg Self-Esteem Scale. Why is this? This is because validity is all about accuracy. We want to be sure the new clinical depression measure does a better job of explaining depression (based on another gold standard in the field, in this case the Beck Depression Inventory) than other closely related but different constructs—anxiety and self-esteem.

So, while this may be starting to sound a little complicated, it doesn't have to be. When you are reading over research, it is not critical that you memorize all of these different tests of validity. Like reliability, most measures of validity are presented in the form of a number that runs from zero to 1, with higher numbers indicating better validity. For you, the key points are that (a) measures are important, (b) these concepts should be addressed in the research you read, and (c) measures of reliability and validity are stronger the closer they get to 1. For the rest, maybe keep this book on your shelf to remind yourself when you need a reminder on the specific types of reliability and validity.

Statistical and Practical Significance of the Outcome

Once you've examined the research design and measurement, the final step is to examine the outcome of the study and determine if it has statistical, practical, and clinical significance for your practice. The first step in this process is to see if there is a statistically significant finding reported between groups at the end of the intervention if there is a control or comparison group or between the pretest and posttest if you're looking at a pre-experimental design. The authors report this in the "Findings" or "Results" section of the article, and they will describe whether there were significant differences between groups or from pretest to posttest in the intervention group. What we mean by significant is that the authors were able to rule out chance or sampling error as an alternative explanation for the relationship between the intervention (intervention vs. control) and the outcome variable(s), or the difference between the pre- and posttest for the same group. If you'd like to know more about this, we encourage you to crack out those old statistics books. If not, please read on. Once you know there was statistically significant change or difference, the key is to know how much of a change or difference there was. This is determined based on effect size, which was covered in Chapter 2 (this volume). The key is to use guidelines of effect size to assess whether the differences between the intervention and the control or comparison group, or an intervention and another intervention, are big enough to warrant their adoption and cost. Once we've done this, it's important to look at the outcome to see what it really means. Many scales, for example, have a clinical cut-off score that determines whether a sample has, on average, gotten below this cut-off score. If the intervention is designed to treat depression, and despite being slightly better than the control group, the average score of the intervention group is still above this cut-off score, then is it really worth adopting? These are some of the important questions to ask when looking at the outcome.

Assessing Applicability, Acceptability of Interventions and Client Preferences to Select an ESI

Once you have found and looked at the research quality and results, the final step in shopping is to narrow down the list of options to the very best one that fits best for the client or target population's background, culture and preferences. It is also important to consider what you or your organization is best able to provide or adopt and implement well. This final step takes a great deal of critical thinking and analyses of these multiple sources of information, as well as checking out the fit of the intervention or program with the client or target population. As mentioned earlier in Chapters 2 and 3 (this volume), the degree to which those receiving the intervention or program buy into the services they receive will have a great impact on their expectancies for it to work and the degree to which they are motivated to engage in what you have to offer.

One way to tackle this is to look at the options you have found in the literature and weigh the available evidence that supports each approach, the fit of each with your client or target population and the ability and resources of you and your agency to offer each option. Consistent with social work values, the next step is to present these treatment or program options with their evidentiary support to your individual client or the target population and see how they sound. When providing interventions at the individual level, this involves informing the client(s) about which options you are trained in or not currently trained in that have evidentiary support. This allows the client to make an informed decision about their options. If you are not able to offer the preferred option, the client should be informed about alternative possibilities where the intervention is delivered locally, if they are available. When you are dealing with making a decision at the organizational level about adopting an intervention to train all of your staff in, it gets a little more complex. In this case, you are not only looking at the fit with your target population, but also whether you can afford the intervention and its training, as well as implement it well with the staff you have.

The costs associated with the adoption of an intervention or program at the agency level can sometimes be cost prohibitive upfront or too expensive to maintain over time. When this is the case, and there are alternative options, the question might be "Which program gives me the best outcomes for the cost?" This is cost-effectiveness. It may be possible to get similar outcomes with a shorter, less complex or costly intervention. For example, one of us has worked on a series of intervention studies—the CHOICES preconception prevention line of research—which has shown that a two-session intervention provided by a master's level clinician is just as effective as a four-session intervention in reducing the risk of alcohol-exposed pregnancy among women of childbearing age. In this case, it is less costly, just as effective and easier to implement the two-session intervention than the four-session intervention (Velasquez et al., 2017). We are now testing the feasibility and comparability of a two-session intervention delivered on a tablet directly to the client as compared to a master's level clinician (Velasquez, Von Sternberg, Stotts, Parrish, & Kowalchuk, 2015). If the tablet has similar results, then this has implications for extending the intervention to agencies where there are fewer resources for training or fidelity monitoring or where staff turnover is high. So, while some interventions or programs may be ideal, contextual issues such as rural location or costs of training may preclude a particular approach. When this is the case, just as when purchasing a car, it is important to keep in mind what an agency can afford and maintain over time. Looking at cost-effectiveness—the cost per positive outcome—and comparing this across interventions can help with this shopping process. It also can help limited resources go much further. Another useful tool is available from the National Implementation Research Network (Metz & Louison, 2018) called "The Hexagon: An Exploration Tool." This tool discussion and analysis tool provides a set of questions and a rating instrument that helps an organization explore potential ESI options with regard to research evidence, usability, supports, programmatic need, capacity, and fit. There are also some helpful questions that can guide this decision at the agency level listed in Figure 5.3. Let's keep these in mind as we utilize the EBP process to shop for the very best ESI in the following example.

Searching for an Evidence Supported Intervention—An Example

Let's suppose you work at a moderately sized nonprofit agency in a large urban area that serves women who have recently experienced interpersonal violence (IPV). Over the last few years, the agency has received many new local referrals and the demographic make-up of the population seems to have changed. To better understand these potential trends, a cursory review of agency records over the last year showed that 80% of women reported identifying as either Hispanic or Latina. Agency records, which included the responses of clients to the PTSD Checklist for DSM-5 (PLC-5) and the Beck Depression Inventory at intake, suggested 60% of women were above the clinical cut-off score for PTSD and 65% were clinically depressed. While your agency has been providing general support groups for women who have recently left their abusive partner, more recent program evaluations and ongoing needs assessments have indicated that this may not be enough to adequately support this population while transitioning out of an abusive relationship. Local funding has become available to fund services to address this need. To ensure that the need is properly defined, your agency conducts a more in-depth needs assessment among the target population and key informants in the community. The results of this needs assessment, which included anonymous surveys, focus groups, and key informant interviews of service providers in the community suggested this population was in need of more specialized mental health services for women who were dealing with trauma, anxiety, and depressive symptoms. It also highlighted the need for services that could address the unique needs within a culturally sensitive and informed lens, primarily for women who were dealing with unique cultural issues from the Latinx community around IPV.

Now that a thorough needs assessment has been conducted, we know what to shop for, just not yet what we will select. Ideally, we want an intervention or program that will be broadly applicable to a largely Latinx population that has experienced IPV and is experiencing mental health symptoms related to trauma, anxiety or depression. The EBP question guiding this process was "What is the most effective intervention for treating PTSD and clinical depression among a primarily Latinx female population who have recently experienced IPV?" Given the lack of knowledge of existing interventions best for the population, predetermined interventions were not included in the EBP question.

Unfortunately, there was not a specific systematic review available that addressed this practice question on the Campbell or Cochrane Collaboration websites, so the next step was to move to Google Scholar to search for meta-analyses. We began our search with terms such as "meta-analysis" and "systematic review" and "intimate partner violence" or "domestic violence" and "women" or "females" and "Hispanic" or "Latina" or "Latinx" and "treatment" and "PTSD" or "depression" or "anxiety." After some reading and refining of search terms, one systematic review and one article using a RCT specific to the targeted population were identified as useful resources. The first was titled "Short-Term Interventions for Survivors of Intimate Partner Violence: A Systematic Review and Meta-Analysis" by Arroyo et al. (2017) and "Posttraumatic Stress Disorder in Latina Women: Examining the Efficacy of the Moms' Empowerment Program" by Galano et al. (2017).

The first meta-analysis, after analyzing 21 selected studies focused on treating trauma, anxiety and depression from IPV, concluded that the most effective interventions were individually delivered CBT approaches specifically tailored to IPV based on IPV theories. Two approaches rose to the top from this synthesis of studies—Cognitive Trauma Therapy for Battered Women With PTSD (CTT-BW; Kubany et al., 2003; 2004) and Helping to Overcome PTSD Through Empowerment (HOPE; Johnson, Zlotnick, & Perez, 2011). These seem to be two potentially promising options, although more information will need to be obtained with regard to availability of materials and cost. While the meta-analysis included studies from diverse samples of women, we also wanted to look for more recent studies that may address this practice issue and, ideally, also fit well with the culture and preferences of the individuals who would be offered services. The previously noted article by Galano et al. focused specifically on PTSD in Latinx women who have experienced IPV. This 10 session group intervention called Moms' Empowerment Program (MEP) aims to treat PTSD among Latinx women by providing a safe, secure environment to share their experiences with IPV, normalize these experiences, increase self-efficacy, and offer social support and access to resources to address legal and financial needs (Galano et al., 2017). Interestingly, the systematic review by Arroyo et al. (2015) did look at the ways in which delivery may impact outcome. With the 21 studies they examined, they found that less brief interventions tended to be more effective and that while both group and individually delivered interventions demonstrated effectiveness, individually delivered interventions were superior to group interventions. So, what do we make of all of this? This is where our critical thinking and consideration of multiple sources of information comes in. Let's start by asking what our options are, shall we?

Option 1: Cognitive Trauma Therapy for Battered Women With PTSD

Pros

CTT-BW has been tested with an ethnically diverse sample of women, replicated in two randomized controlled studies with significant differences between groups, and PTSD remitting in 87% of participants in the intervention group in the second study and 30 of 32 participants in the first study (Kubany et al., 2003, 2004). This intervention is relatively short with only 8 to 11 individual sessions. There is a detailed description of CTT-BW—a manual of sorts—in an article titled "Cognitive Trauma Therapy for Formerly Battered Women with PTSD: Conceptual Bases and Treatment Outcomes (Kubany & Watson, 2002). Within this manual, the authors also recommend outcome measures to collect to assess improvement of your clients over time.

Cons

This would likely require intensive training in interpersonal violence issues for staff—at the very least licensed master's level staff to provide the intervention. It will also be more expensive to provide individual services compared to group services. This intervention is not directly tailored to the specific Latinx community being served.

Option 2: Helping to Overcome PTSD Through Empowerment (HOPE)

Pros

HOPE includes diverse sample of women experiencing IPV, although only 4.3% Hispanic. Provided in the shelter in the context of a supportive milieu and other support groups. The HOPE intervention provided, above and beyond these services, eight weeks of psychoeducational information focused on safety, cognitions, triggers, self-soothing, boundaries, anger management, and support systems (Johnson, Zlotnick, & Perez, 2011). While there was not a difference between groups with regard to PTSD diagnosis overall, the treatment group had a greater reduction of emotional numbing symptoms and a lower incidence of re-abuse. There does not appear to be a manual available online, but if you were interested in this option, the developers of this intervention did a nice job describing the intervention in this reference—"HOPE for Battered Women With PTDS in Domestic Violence Shelters" (Johnson & Zlotnick, 2009). It is also possible to contact them with interest in replicating the intervention to see if they would provide you with their manual and advice for adopting and implementing the intervention.

Cons

The intervention group was not more effective than treatment as usual in treating PTSD. It also may be that for this intervention to be effective, it has to be delivered within a supportive shelter milieu. This not part of the services provided by your agency, which primarily offers support services and case management during the daytime hours. This intervention has not been used primarily with an ethnically similar population as the one our agency will be working with. There may be issues with regard to cultural relevance and fit.

Option 3: Moms' Empowerment Program (MEP)

Pros

This intervention was developed specifically to treat PTSD for Latinx women (Spanish-speaking) who have experienced IPV, but it has also been effective among white and African American low-income women. MEP was developed by noting that "the ability to name and talk about past violent experiences (exposure therapy) and to receive psychoeducation is an important element of these successful programs" for Latina women (Galano et al., 2017, p. 346). It also highlights the cultural relevance of connection to community and social support valued in Latina populations that comes from peer group discussion in the context of group treatment from prior research. Finally, women are supported with additional legal, housing, and financial services and resources in the community. Overall, the MEP intervention group had significantly reduced PTSD symptoms compared to the control group, but with regard to PTSD symptomology, the significant difference was focused on re-experiencing rather than avoidance or hyperarousal. MEP has been disseminated and described with further details on the National Institutes of Justice website (https://www. crimesolutions.gov/ProgramDetails.aspx?ID=579). There is also detailed information on how and who is currently implementing this program on the National Center on Domestic Violence as well as the key contact person for more information in obtaining the manual (http://www.nationalcenterdvtraumamh. org/wp-content/uploads/2019/04/NCDVTMH_TIInterventions_Graham-BermannSummary.pdf).

Cons

This approach utilizes a group format approach that may more culturally relevant, yet less effective than offering an individualized, tailored approach to treatment that utilizes techniques more in line with CBT to reach broader PTSD symptoms per the Arroyo et al. (2015) meta-analysis. One important consideration is that this program was developed specifically for women who are already moms. It is very possible that this agency serves Hispanic or Latinx women who are not mothers. If only this program is selected, what services will be provided for women who are not moms? Would this program be appropriate for them?

Making a Choice

Now that your agency has these options, what do you do? What are your first thoughts about how to proceed? This is Step 4—integrating the best available research evidence with your clinical expertise, organizational mission, and resources, and the client fit and preferences come in to play. Since all three options have empirical support, the next question to consider is what is the best fit with your agency and target population's needs? This is where not only critical thinking, but the art—yes, the art—of EBP happens. If we look back at your agency's demographics, 80% identify as Hispanic or Latina. A more detailed look at agency demographics shows that 90% of Latinx women experiencing IPV are also mothers and that 70% of the remaining 20% women served are also mothers. This means many of these women are mothers, so the MEP program could be a potentially viable, culturally sensitive program. HOPE, in contrast, does not seem to be a good fit given its delivery primarily within a shelter setting that offered additional milieu support services.

Your organization decides to conduct a couple of focus groups with women who are representative of those served to assess the views of the CTT-BW and MEP interventions by describing each and asking them whether they would be likely to participate, why and why not, and whether they believe this kind of service is needed. You also hold several meetings with administrators and practitioners in your agency to discuss these options. In the end, based on this feedback from both the focus groups and your agency staff, you decide to explore the adoption of both the CTT-BW and MEP programs, as this would offer women the choice of intervention that seems to be the best fit based on their preferences and individual needs based on IPV-related trauma, depression, and anxiety symptoms. Adopting both programs may also allow some women in need of both intensive individual support and social support the opportunity to benefit from both options together. The next step would involve contacting the developers of each intervention to obtain available training materials to explore the program in greater detail and better estimate the cost of the programs and whether there is enough funding to offer both. Now that you have shopped and narrowed down your ESI options, the next step is to make a final decision to adopt one or both interventions—Step 5 of the EBP process—and then implement them well so that your clients will have the very best chance to benefit from these programs. We will focus on that in the next chapter. While we will focus quite a bit on implementation in this book, it's also important to remember that it is important to both implement the intervention well *and* evaluate the outcomes of the selected intervention (Step 6 of the EBP process).

Preparing for Challenges in the ESI Shopping Process

After using these tips to identify your ESI, you may end up with some options that end up not being feasible due to cost, a lack of training, or some other challenge to adoption. The very best research may support the use of an intervention that is too expensive or too difficult to implement given the agency's staffing, setting, or resources. The agency or staff may not be ready or willing to implement a particular intervention, and it may take time to convince them that it is a good fit—or they may never agree. You may not find enough research evidence to answer your practice question. This is rarer now than in years past with the development and testing of many different social work relevant interventions. However, it is possible. In this case, perhaps cast the net broader in your literature search or think about theoretically and empirically driven adaptation of interventions. We'll discuss that process in Chapter 6 (this volume).

If you are fortunate enough to have found something great and can feasibly implement it, there is more work ahead. Very few interventions are implemented as intended in real-world settings, which make it more difficult to achieve the same strong effects as those obtained in high quality RCTs. In the next chapter, we will provide an overview implementation. Whether you choose to implement a well-researched intervention or develop one yourself, an implementation strategy is critical to making sure that the intervention is delivered as it was intended.

Discussion Questions

1. What are some of the qualities of studies that reside at the top of the intervention hierarchy (systematic reviews, meta-analyses, and RCTs) that make them stronger than studies lower on the hierarchy?
2. How can you determine whether a study is using good measures to assess outcomes?
3. What is the difference between statistical and practical or clinical significance of an outcome?
4. If you cannot identify an ESI, what other options do you have to implement an intervention?

5

Implementation Overview

In recent years intervention developers, the federal government, and proponents of evidence-based practice (EBP) among others have figured out that you can't just build an intervention and expect people to use it. Even wonderful interventions with fantastic outcomes sometimes do not get used very often in practice. So why? What is going on when the best available research evidence supports an intervention, but its application in practice is limited or is poorly done? What can be done about this? These are the questions of implementation science. If EBP is in its adolescence, implementation science is in its infancy. New research on how to best support implementation is continuously developed.

Implementation science builds on the EBP process. The idea is that you find some research evidence supporting alternative interventions, you weigh that evidence in the context of resources, client preferences, and other constraints—and then you just do it! Simple, right? It took the field of EBP some time to get around to understanding what practitioners have long known. Telling people "just do it" does little to actually get interventions into practice. Even if there is an intervention that rises above the others in terms of the strength of the research evidence, implementation of an intervention is complex. *Disseminating* information about a good intervention may improve people's knowledge of or perceptions about an intervention, but it won't get them to change their behavior.

The Loss of Intervention Potency from Research to Practice

Studies have demonstrated that when interventions are moved from the strictly controlled and well-resourced research environments to more real-world practice settings, outcomes are often disappointing. An evidence-supported intervention (ESI) with medium to large effect sizes in a randomized controlled trial may only evidence small effect sizes when used in usual practice. This has

---

Box 5.1

Studies have demonstrated that when interventions are moved from the strictly controlled and well-resourced research environments to more real-world practice settings, outcomes are often disappointing.

---

certainly been true in our work. As we mentioned in Chapter 2, one of us has been working with a team of researchers to develop a new home-visiting intervention that is designed to better serve fathers called Dads Matter-HV. Our research team conducted a small study with about 20 families that showed very promising results. We showed large effect sizes across many outcomes. But when we rolled out the intervention to a larger group of families, the effect sizes weren't as impressive. What accounts for this?

There are a lot of explanations for this loss of potency. In some cases, it may be that there is some bias introduced in the research study. For example, oftentimes intervention developers test their own interventions, and intervention developers have a vested interested in seeing their intervention succeed. Having an intervention developer study their own intervention is somewhat like asking a parent to rate the abilities of their own child. In this analogy, the intervention developer is the parent, and the intervention is their baby. There is a great deal of time and energy invested in producing pilot work, conceptual models, and other foundational elements of interventions. We can tell you this from personal experience. We are *very* attached to the interventions we develop and support. Unfortunately, biases can influence research studies in subtle ways that may affect research outcomes and overblow the results. Many researchers work hard to reduce these biases by using research techniques. However, bias can easily sneak into a study.

For example, one of us is working on a study right now in which the research team must frequently make decisions about whether to keep a client in the study when something goes wrong. This study is a randomized controlled trial, so we are comparing our team's intervention against someone else's. One of the things we're interested in improving is the quality of parenting. Sometimes we receive a referral into the study for a parent who just barely misses some eligibility criteria. Commonly, in our study, the child is just barely a little older than the ones we're hoping to include. We know that as parents who have more experience in their parenting career, and as children get a little older, it gets a little bit harder to change a more seasoned parent's behavior. If we know that this parent is in the intervention group, it would be in my interest to go ahead and exclude them. Why? Because if we leave them in the intervention group, even though their behaviors are harder to change, it will drag down the average performance of the intervention. On the flip side, if they are in the control group, we may be tempted to keep them in because that will drag down the control group outcomes and potentially make the intervention look better by comparison.

Bias isn't the only explanation for the difference in outcomes we see in research studies versus real-world practice settings. Figure 5.1 lists some of the other reasons. Another big concern is fidelity to the model. Remember the cautionary tale of motivational interviewing (MI)? If people don't do MI correctly, they cannot expect to get outcomes that are as strong as those in the research studies. Also, it can be very expensive and time-consuming to obtain training, manuals, and certification in many different ESIs. Some of the most efficacious interventions can cost several thousand dollars to deliver per client. In addition, it can be very difficult to access training resources for some ESIs, and even if they are obtained, processes need to be in place to ensure that competency in delivering the ESI is maintained with staff turnover.

Yet other interventions have been developed, tested, and demonstrated to produce promising results but do not have any training structure or capacity. So, you can read about them and all the wonderful potential they hold, but it may be all but impossible to actually get your hands on the tools and training needed to use the intervention to its best effect in practice. All of these challenges might result in practitioners only using parts or pieces of the ESI or just reading about it and trying to perform the intervention without spending the time and resources to get certified or maintain certification.

Interventions vary a great deal in terms of cost, ease of accessing manuals, training, and certification. In the case of MI, it is actually relatively inexpensive to purchase training materials and manuals. The main MI book can be purchased at any bookstore, many training resources are available nationally (e.g., Tip 35: Enhancing Motivation for Change in Substance Use Treatment on

---

Researchers may introduce bias into their studies that favor the outcomes that they want to see. This is more often a concern when intervention developers test their own intervention.

ESIs are often tested with groups of people who may not reflect the diverse clients served in practice, including clients that have more complicating factors or higher risk.

Research studies used to establish the efficacy of ESIs are often more well-resourced than the programs and providers available in the community. Practitioners in the field don't get adequate training, oversight, supervision, or oth supports designed to make sure the intervention is delivered as intended.

Figure 5.1 Reasons why interventions may perform better in studies than in practice.

the Substance Abuse and Mental Health Services Administration website), and there is a network of trainers (Motivational Interviewing Network of Trainers, or MINTees), that can be quite affordable to hire to do brief trainings locally or play a consultative role to practitioners or organizations that wish to implement this particular MI. You can also google "Motivational Interviewing" and a variety of local resources are also likely to come up. Unfortunately, it is this ease of access that has caused the developers some difficulty as many people accessed these widely available materials and trainings and reported that they were delivering MI, when in fact their skills and ability to implement MI as it was intended were inadequate. What is worse, studies began to emerge questioning the overall effectiveness of this intervention, when in fact the problem was that folks just weren't delivering MI, but rather something else. The truth is that it takes a commitment to training, coaching, and skill development to deliver MI appropriately.

The problem of interventions getting away from the quality control of developers is of great concern to intervention developers who do not want people to poorly implement their interventions only to claim that it didn't work. This lack of quality control is also of great concern to the practitioners, organizations, and service systems who invest a lot of time and money in training and supports only to be disappointed by the results. And most problematic, the delivery of poor-quality services is of great concern to clients and communities won't reap the potential benefits that might've been realized had they received the intervention as it was designed to be delivered. As social workers, we are privileged to provide services to some of the highly vulnerable people and communities. We owe it to them to deliver the best interventions we can to the best of our abilities.

So, when interventions do not work in the field, we have to ask, Was it because the intervention didn't work for my particular clients or in my particular context? Was it because the research study was biased toward the researchers' preferred outcome? Or was it because the intervention was delivered to the standards needed to achieve comparable outcomes? Sometimes it can be hard to tell, but we are going to take on each of these issues in subsequent chapters and discuss some of the strategies that can be used to anticipate, assess, and manage these challenges so that you get the best possible results when you implement an intervention.

What Is Implementation?

If we were to ask this question "What is implementation?" just ten years ago, very few social work researchers would have been able to answer it. In fact, when one of the authors shared with her doctoral program director an interest in implementation and dissemination science as a part of her future research agenda just 10 years ago, he strongly discouraged her because he had never heard of it and didn't think anyone else had either. The truth is, the concept of implementation as it relates to successfully installing empirically supported interventions in real-world settings is fairly new across various helping fields including social work, public health, medicine, and psychology. Despite its infancy, it is a rapidly growing field that had garnered much wider support given the realization that it takes nearly 17 years to translate efficacious interventions into real practice settings (Morris, Wooding, & Grant, 2011), and the rare full-scale implementation of interventions and programs with fidelity in real settings. As the field has grown, there has been a proliferation of emerging theory, models, and frameworks to guide both research and practice concerning guiding the effective implementation of empirically supported interventions. So where to start? Let's start by trying to answer our first question: What is implementation? To truly understand this, we need to provide you with some historical context and define a few terms that lay the groundwork for understanding the concept of implementation.

Implementation was born out of the perfect storm. On one hand, there was a growing recognition and concern about the lack and lag of translation of well-funded empirically supported interventions or programs into real practice settings among many stakeholders, including federal funding sources (e.g., National Institutes of Health, Substance Abuse and Mental Health Services Administration; Glasglow et al., 2012). On the other hand, there were some pioneering researchers who were already perplexed about this and actively working to identifying theory or practices that could better illuminate approaches or processes to improve the adoption and implementation of these ESIs in the real world. This group of researchers, who founded the National Implementation Research Network (NIRN), released a comprehensive review of the implementation research literature in the mid-2000s (Fixsen, Naoom, Blase, Friedman, & Wallace, 2005; National Implementation Research Network, 2016). This review, which drew upon Rogers's *Diffusion of Innovations Theory* (Rogers, 2003), reported on many key elements to consider when maximizing the success of the diffusion, adoption, and implementation of ESIs. Rogers's theory provided an especially useful lens when considering the ESI as the innovation that had not yet been adopted by agencies, practitioners, or even policymakers. It helped explain why it takes some organizations so little time—the early adopters—to seek to implement ESIs compared to the laggards (don't you love that term?) who took much, much longer. From this point forward and largely based on this seminal synthesis of the literature, Fixsen et al. (2005) and many others have proposed dissemination and implementation models to guide the practical implementation of ESIs and the evaluation of this implementation process. Yes, we know we have not yet told you what implementation is yet, but it's comingwe promise!

The State of Implementation in the Field

Today, there are well over 100 dissemination and implementation models that have been disseminated (see Tabak et al., 2012), so there is not enough time or space for us to cover them all. And we wouldn't want to do that, as the field is now already inundated with too many models and too much terminology, so much that even the experts get confused by it all (Nilsen, 2015). To reduce this confusion and make this chapter most meaningful, we are going to provide a you with a brief description of the most commonly used models and then introduce our favorite one—the one we think is most usable and informative—in detail. But, before we start, let's provide you with a few simple definitions that help us better understand what we mean and don't mean when we use the term implementation. And then we'll tell you what implementation is!

First, there is the concept of *diffusion*, which is what happens when ESIs are spread without any intentional marketing or planning. This is a sort of haphazard process whereby interventions are picked up and used by practitioners who happen to hear about the intervention through colleagues, maybe in school during their training, or maybe at a conference. Historically, intervention developers would often develop, test, and write about interventions in professional journals and present their findings at conferences. Because few practitioners regularly read the scientific journals in which researchers publish their work, and oftentimes practitioners and researchers attend different conferences, many useful studies about effective interventions never made it into the hands of those who might most benefit from them.

The burden really has most often been on practitioners to find interventions, including those that are supported by research evidence, choose to use them, and then support the uptake of the intervention in practice. This burden is part of the reason why the spread and quality of ESIs is so uneven across states, localities, and organizations. The infrastructure necessary for full and widespread implementation just hasn't been there. To be fair, as intervention developers we got a lot of training on how to test an intervention and write about it, and absolutely no training in how to actually scale up and implement interventions across a large number of practitioners or organizations. Researchers like us, who are based in universities, aren't often rewarded for partnering with social service providers to implement interventions. We are rewarded for publishing papers about our interventions and securing more grants to develop and test them. This too limits implementation.

Dissemination, in contrast, is the active and planned sharing of ESIs. Although dissemination is an upgrade from diffusion, it really only involves efforts to persuade target groups to adopt a new intervention. Dissemination strategies are things like using brochures or marketing. One popular and highly regarded dissemination option at one time was the National Registry of Evidence-Based Programs and Practices. In 2018, the U.S. Assistant Secretary of Mental Health and Substance Use decided to remove this website from public access. This online registry and decision tool was widely used for disseminating ESIs to the practice community, with firm criteria for inclusion based on research evidence and opportunities to provide implementation support tools and additional information for decision making all in one place. Researchers and others who had invested in the development of this resource were widely discouraged by this decision (Green-Henessy, 2018). The reason for pulling this registry down (and not replacing it with anything still to this day) was that there was not sufficient "rigor or breadth" of programs and the perceived need that this registry should be replaced with an Evidence-Based Practices Resources Center that houses agency practice guidelines to guide practice (Green-Henessy, 2018). In time, practitioners and researchers will need to decide if this more authoritative and nondirect approach to dissemination is acceptable.

Even if dissemination is successful, it does not necessarily mean an ESI will be *adopted.* Whether an ESI is adopted by an organization depends on many factors, some of which have to do with the organization's readiness to adopt new innovations and others of which are ideally based on information highlighted in the EBP process, including the best available research evidence, the fit of the intervention or program with the client population, the availability of materials to support adoption, and the expertise and feasibility of the organization to implement the program. We're back to that implementation word! Yes, once an ESI has been diffused or disseminated and then officially adopted, *implementation* includes the systematic application of purposeful activities to bring an ESI to full scale with regard to quality and effectiveness in real practice settings (Eccles & Mittman, 2006; Fixsen et al., 2005). As you will see soon, there are many considerations and supports necessary for making this happen.

Implementation Models

Now that you're more familiar with what implementation is, we'll share a little more about the models that are available to guide the implementation process. One way to understand the emergence of these many models is to understand the ways they have been classified. Two model categories are of interest here— determinant frameworks and evaluation frameworks (Nilsen, 2015). These are both of interest as they are both concerned with identifying if and, if so, how an implementation effort has been successful. *Determinant frameworks* identify determinants—both barriers and enablers—that influence implementation success, and some even specify the relationships between these determinants. Determinant frameworks also are similar in that they take a systems approach to understanding how implementation works, with a focus on each subsystem within the integrated whole and the interdependent relationships between them (Nilsen, 2015). Hmmm—sounds a little bit like social work!

Two common determinant implementation frameworks include Promoting Action on Research Implementation in Health (Kitson et al., 2008) and Active Implementation Frameworks (Blase, Van Dyke, Fixsen, & Bailey, 2012; Fixsen, Blase, Metz, & Van Dyke, 2015). Promoting Action on Research Implementation in Health initially emerged as an observation of what successful healthcare implementation looked like, which was proposed to be characteristics of evidence, context, and facilitation. These concepts have subsequently been developed and widely applied in health contexts; however, there remains a need for further study (Helfrich et al., 2010). Active Implementation Frameworks (also formerly called Stages of Implementation and Core Implementation Components) were built off of and from the aforementioned comprehensive review of the literature that originated with the NIRN in the mid-2000s (Fixsen et al., 2005) and the experience of these authors in conducting implementation research studies (Blase et al., 2012; Fixsen et al., 2015). We will not describe this approach here, as this is the model we will be describing and applying in detail later in the chapter. We have selected this as our guiding model for this text given the number of useful online tools and guidance the NIRN has historically made freely available to the field and its comprehensive systems focus for informing the ESI implementation process. We will draw broadly on their work in the text, but we strongly encourage you to explore their website for more information and useful tools (http://nirn.fpg.unc.edu/).

The *evaluation frameworks* are specifically developed to provide guidance for evaluating the outcomes of an implementation effort. However, it is important to point out that the determinant frameworks can also be used to guide evaluation of implementation efforts as well, given there are well operationalized concepts guiding these models as well. There are two widely used evaluation frameworks we will briefly describe. The first is the Reach Effectiveness Adoption Implementation Maintenance (RE-AIM; Glasgow et al., 1999) model. RE-AIM is designed to evaluate the public health impact of an ESI as a function of its reach, efficacy, adoption, implementation and maintenance (Glasgow et al., 1999). This was one of the first implementation frameworks disseminated, with over 100 studies published using this framework (Beidas, Mehta, Atkins, Solomon, & Merz, 2013). At the individual level, reach describes the proportion of individuals who need a program who receive it while efficacy refers to how well it works. At the community or policy level, adoption describes the number of settings that decide to implement the ESI, whereas implementation is the extent to which it is installed as intended. Maintenance is the extent to which the ESI is sustained and becomes a culture of the individual and organization level contexts. Each of these five factors is rated on a scale of zero to 100, with the total score representing the public health impact. These scores can be used to plot and compare various ESIs with regard to their broad implementation outcomes.

The second implementation evaluation framework was developed by a social worker, Enola Proctor and her colleagues (Proctor et al., 2011). While it does not have a fancy name like the other frameworks, it has played a pivotal role in helping to drive the implementation field forward in better conceptualizing and operationalizing implementation outcomes. This model—which some refer to as the Conceptual Model of Implementation Research—based on Proctor's original implementation framework (Proctor et al., 2009) and a review of the existing implementation literature—describes and defines eight conceptually distinct implementation outcomes for the field: acceptability, adoption, appropriateness, feasibility, fidelity, implementation cost, penetration, and sustainability. Some of these concepts may sound a little repetitive at this point. If they do, that's OK, as that is the current state of literature right now and they are important concepts. Generally, we all pretty much agree on the important elements of implementation. It's just that the field grew so rapidly with many people thinking and proposing similar ideas at the same time that we now need to figure out how to get on the same page to build this knowledge base together moving forward. That's why Proctor's contribution to the literature is so important.

So, at this point, you may be asking yourself, Why is it important to focus on implementation outcomes *and* program outcomes? Think about this, if you are responsible for running a new program, maybe even one that has been developed by you or your agency, you need to have some approaches in place to make certain that you and your colleagues are doing the intervention right. If you don't know if you're doing it correctly or well, how do you even know that you're actually evaluating the intervention itself? You might have picked the very best ESI for your agency and then, because you did not implement it well, think it was not effective when it really could have been. Also, even if you get it set up correctly at first, there is a tendency over time for interventions to drift away from their original design. So, when we talk about implementation, we're not only talking about how to train folks to do an intervention correctly, we're also talking how to keep them doing an intervention correctly over time. This is called *maintenance*, and maintenance is hard.

We will give you another example from our work in training home visitors to use a new intervention. At the beginning of the randomized controlled trial through which we were testing the effectiveness of Dads Matter-HV, we brought together home visitors and their supervisors and provided them with an introductory, one-day training. We followed this training up with clinical supervision phone calls with supervisors and in-person meetings with the staff who were delivering the intervention. In the beginning, it seemed that home visitors were using Dads Matter-HV and participating in these activities to learn how to use the intervention to its best advantage. But, over time, participation seemed to wane. Supervisors seemed less likely to participate in clinical supervision calls or didn't seem as engaged with case examples and questions. Our fidelity data suggested that home visitors were only using parts of the intervention.

There are lots of things that can account for this process. When we talked with staff about what was going on, here are some of the answers we got back:

> "We're just busy. It's hard to find the time to do Dads Matter-HV when we have all of these other requirements to meet."
> "The intervention doesn't really fit very well for us."
> "I just don't want to work with fathers."
> "My supervisor didn't tell me we still had to do it."

Each of these statements points to different problems that can eat away at the maintenance of an intervention. Time and competing demands, a lack of buy-in to the value of the intervention, personal biases, or unclear expectations. Home visitors felt fatigued by the effort to implement Dads Matter-HV and not always well-supported in their efforts to continue to use the intervention and increase their skills.

One important goal of implementation is getting the intervention integrated into the standards of usual practice so that the intervention and the processes that support its correct use are highly integrated into the everyday structures and processes of the agency that is delivering the intervention. Some home-visiting teams were better able to achieve this goal by making Dads Matter-HV assessments part of the standard intake process, scheduling time to talk about the intervention during each and every group supervision meeting, and integrating intervention-related data collection and reporting tools into the required paperwork of the staff. These strategies kept the intervention on the front burner, conveyed the expectation that delivery of the new intervention is expected and required, and underscored that its consistent and proper use is a priority to the agency. Every effort to implement an intervention is likely to result in some similar challenges. And, anticipating these challenges and putting into place tools and approaches to anticipate and address them should be part of the implementation process.

1. Pre-assessement to determine whether or not users have the necessary resources to implement the intervention

2. Manuals, books, or other supporting materials that direct how the intervention should be done in practice

3. Training to convey the skills needed to successfully begin to implement the intervention

4. Coaching and consultation to support the ongoing development and maintenance of skills needed to implement the intervention

5. Fidelity monitoring to ensure that the intervention is being implemented with a high level of quality

Figure 5.2 Supports, tools, and processes that support implementation.

Common Implementation Supports, Tools, and Processes

Most efforts to support implementation have come from intervention developers or the groups that have been developed to support the implementation of specific ESIs. Intervention developers vary a great deal in terms of the relationship that they maintain with the implementation process. In some cases, the only way to get training and certification is directly from the person who created the intervention. In other cases, an entirely separate organization has been created that is designed to focus on the implementation of the ESI. These intermediary groups are sometimes called intervention purveyors.

We will review some of the most common processes and supports that have been developed by intervention developers or their partner organizations to facilitate the implementation of ESI. Some ESIs require that practitioners who want to use their interventions participate in every single one of these components, while other might require only a few or none at all. Even if you don't plan to use an ESI, but perhaps will instead develop or support another intervention, these components outlined in Figure 5.2 still serve to make sure that you can implement and maintain the intervention to a high standard.

Pre-assessment

Increasingly ESIs require that practitioners or organizations participate in some sort of pre-assessment to determine if they have the appropriate resources, such as staff, credentials, meeting space, or funding, in place to properly support the intervention. In some cases, these pre-assessments are submitted to the intervention developer or their implementation team for review. In other cases, a tool may be provided to guide practitioners or organizations in determining whether or not they have the resources necessary to support the intervention before beginning implementation. If the resources are not yet in place, these tools also can inform your efforts to seek funding to support a new program. Some ESI even include cost planning tools that specify the exact costs associated with training, manuals, consultation, assessments, or other resources. These tools can clarify what is needed to implement and support the intervention's implementation.

Manuals, Books, or Other Supporting Materials

ESIs must have some sort of manual, book, or other materials that guide practice. Some interventions may include a curriculum with specific assessment tools, activities, discussion guides, or other components. These materials are used to help communicate the components of the intervention to service providers. Even if an intervention has not had the benefit of rigorous studies to support its use in practice, these materials are needed to make sure that the intervention is being done correctly by those who are using it whether you are supervising practitioners, or using the intervention yourself. Recall one of the most common reasons that interventions achieve disappointing outcomes in practice is that the intervention is not being done properly.

Some manuals and other materials are available for download from an intervention website, whereas others are in paper or other formats—increasingly videos and other types of technology might be available to provide guidance as to how to actually use the intervention in practice. These materials vary greatly in price and in quality. When you are considering using an ESI, it can be extremely helpful to examine these materials. However, it can also be difficult for you to get your hands on these things before paying for them.

We'll tell you a little story about this very problem. Not too long ago, one of us was trying to compare the components of different parent training interventions to examine how "father friendly" each one was. First, this was an expensive proposition. Some manuals and materials for certain ESI cost well over $2,000. A small grant was actually required just to purchase these things. In other cases, the manual was not available for purchase unless someone from the organization went to a training. This was prohibitively expensive and time-consuming for a junior professor. So, we reached out to colleagues who had been trained in the intervention and to find anyone who had a manual that could be borrowed. In one case, no manual could be found. Even worse, there was no way to contact the intervention developers. After a lot of frustration and failed networking and sleuthing, it turns out that the intervention developers had retired and didn't leave any way for practitioners to get access to the supporting materials or training for their intervention. It was a shame too, because it sounded like it was pretty father-friendly!

Because some intervention developers, or their organizations, charge a fee for these materials to support their work and continued development of improvements to the ESI or even to support the development of other interventions, there can be restrictions placed on what material can be shared and under what conditions. These materials are often copyrighted and protected. In other cases, when the intervention developer has not built an infrastructure to support the dissemination of their ESI, the only way to access these materials may be to contact them directly. Increasingly organizations that identify and review ESI also provide information about implementation quality and supports so that you don't have to do all the detective work. Groups like the California Evidence-Based Clearinghouse for Child Welfare provide details on the availability of manuals, training, and even costs.

Training

ESIs, or really any programs that have been disseminated with or without research evidence, most often include some sort of opportunity for training. Many ESI will include a series of trainings that increase in sophistication, required time, and cost. For example, The Incredible Years (IY) is a well-regarded ESI with a website that includes a lot of information about how to access the resources and materials necessary for implementing the intervention, including information about training options. In this model, there are two- to three-day introductory trainings to become an IY group leader, as well as additional training, peer coaching, and evaluation to become an IY coach, mentor, or trainer. ESI often have these multilevel training models, which frequently start with a one- to three-day introduction, often in a group format. This training may or may not be sufficient to actually start using the intervention. In the case of IY, the intervention developers state that this training is not required but has been shown to improve outcomes.

Much like the cost and availability of manuals and other supporting materials, access to training can also vary greatly across different intervention models. In some cases, you may be required to travel to a training center or other location to receive the training. In other cases, you may be able to hire a trainer to provide training to you or your staff at your organization. In some more well-disseminated models, local trainers may be available. Access to training has been a common barrier to the widespread implementation of ESIs. The problem is even more pronounced in certain areas, such as rural communities that may not have access to local trainers and face more challenges in traveling to offsite locations. Increasingly online training and materials are available, but it is not often the case that you can become fully trained and certified in a sophisticated ESI completely in the online environment.

Coaching and Consulting

Some ESIs require some type of coaching or consultation to be certified to provide the intervention. After you have completed some initial training, many ESI require that you apply your skills with a certain number of clients and have that application of skills observed. The duration and method of observation also varies quite a bit. In most cases, you will be asked to either audio or video record your use of the ESI with a certain number of clients or with a certain number of groups. Oftentimes these recordings are sent to a consultant who will review the recording, rate the skill with which the intervention is delivered, and provide feedback to the practitioner. In other cases, a consultant or trainer might observe the practitioner trainee as they attempt to use the ESI rather than assessing a recording.

This whole idea of observation as part of training sometimes gives practitioners the heebie-jeebies. Social workers are rarely asked to record their work or allow others to observe them working with a client, particularly after they have been practicing for some time. This was definitely the case for us! One of us used to work at a crisis counseling center that included taking calls from students who were struggling with stress, break-ups, chronic mental health problems, or suicidal thoughts. Never knowing who would be on the line or what the call would bring was nerve-wracking and time-pressured. Even in less pressured scenarios, you might think to yourself, "Jeez, if I just had a moment to think straight, I would have said something different, asked a different question, or directed the discussion along a different path." At the crisis center, we had the ability to record our interactions with callers using an audio recorder linked up to the telephone line. But this was optional, and hardly anyone ever pushed the record button. Part of this, we think is due to training. For one of us, our introduction to recorded observation was being videotaped exactly one time during the master's program to learn basic interviewing and assessment skills, and it was *miserable*. Watching yourself, hearing every "um," "ah," and "well" that used to fill the uncomfortable silence can be tough. It was intimidating and if you only do it once, or a few times, you will never get over the discomfort. More ideally, if audiotaping, videotaping, and observation are the norm, we might have less resistance to this approach. Although workers at the crisis center rarely pushed the record button, when they did it was incredibly helpful to hear them apply their clinical skills in supervision. And, honestly, the most helpful recordings were those that went wrong. Where the caller hung up, or the session went nowhere. Those are the opportunities to learn and reflect.

In addition, some ESIs provide or require either in-person or telephone consultation as well. These consultation sessions might be where feedback is provided based on the observations, or where practitioners simply get the chance to ask questions or talk about their application of the intervention in practice. In many cases, this consultation might be provided for a limited amount of time, perhaps until the practitioner has achieved a certain level of mastery. But, in other cases, the consultation may be required to maintain certification indefinitely. Either way, consultation is rarely free and should be another cost to consider and factor in when you are thinking about implementing an ESI.

Fidelity Monitoring

Most ESIs have some type of approach to monitoring fidelity to the intervention over time. As a reminder, fidelity is the degree to which the ESI is being provided as intended. Frequently ESI have fidelity tools that practitioners can use to check their own use of the intervention or use in supervision to make sure their staff are providing the intervention as intended. For example, most studies of MI, and even some agencies (Crouch & Parrish, 2015) utilize the Motivational Interviewing Treatment Integrity 3.1.1—a behavioral coding system—to monitor fidelity of MI and provide feedback to practitioners in the field via coaching to improve practice in nonresearch settings. For example, Cathy Crouch, a social worker, MINT trainer and executive vice president of SEARCH Homeless Services, trains her bachelor's and master's level case managers in MI through ongoing trainings, coaching, and feedback (Crouch & Parrish, 2015). To accomplish this, she has served as the agency champion and opinion leader for empirically supported and data-driven approaches. However, we know that this degree of implementation effort is rare in most agencies. Monitoring fidelity can be as simple as using a checklist-type tool or may be much more sophisticated in nature, perhaps including periodic observations or other quality benchmarks. We will discuss fidelity in much more detail in Chapter 9 (this volume).

Factors and Drivers That Support Implementation

Aside from these processes and tools that can support the implementation of high-quality intervention, researchers have identified other factors that can increase the likelihood that a new policy, program, or practice is implemented with a high degree of quality.

Some of the factors that have an impact on implementation are out of your control. For example, one of the characteristics that impacts implementation is the simplicity of the intervention. An intervention that is relatively easy to use and straightforward is more likely to be implemented with success (Bach-Mortensen, Lange, & Montgomery, 2018). This makes some good intuitive sense. Likely this is because practitioners may not elect to use an intervention because it sounds too complicated, the resources required might be too burden-some, or the intervention might be too difficult to sustain over the long haul.

Some interventions designed to help some of the most vulnerable populations and intractable problems are pretty complex. For example, assertive community treatment (ACT) involves sophisticated case management techniques that in-volve the collaboration of multiple professionals over a long period of time to support people with serious and persistent mental illness. As a service provider, there is likely little you can do to change this model without risking the possi-bility that it will no longer work well. So, what can you do? One solution is to work with your colleagues to better understand the model before you imple-ment it. Despite its complexity, there are some relatively simple tenets at its core. Likely, the implementation of an ACT team will not feel as overwhelming once you become familiar with the overarching concepts and components. It might also make sense to talk with other practitioners who have used ACT teams to get their recommendations as to how they addressed issues related to resource limi-tations or other challenges that flow from its complexity. In other cases, you just may not have the capacity to support such a sophisticated intervention.

You can also think about leveraging other factors that are supportive of imple-mentation to balance out the challenges that are less amenable to change. For ex-ample, practitioners who see a real value or payoff in using a new intervention are more likely to implement that intervention well (Fixsen et al., 2005). Sometimes this just means making the improvements or benefits more obvious or clear. Here's another story for you. One of us worked with a social service agency that was interested in implementing a relatively brief telephone intervention that was designed to reduce their no-show rate. This agency, like lots of social service agencies, was plagued by high no-show rates. Clients would make appointments but wouldn't keep them—something like half of the appointments were no-shows. This is not only irritating; it is also costly. That time slot that could have been used to bill for staff time is lost, and other clients are forced to join ever growing wait lists. So, this is a big problem. After reviewing the literature, the in-tervention that we came up with, which was informed by research evidence, was to call clients approximately 48 hours before their appointment to (a) confirm and (b) find out if there were any barriers that we could address that might make it hard for them to attend the appointment. This had the benefit of serving as a reminder, removing common barriers like transportation since the agency could

1. **Competency Drivers:** coaching, training, staffing
2. **Organizational Drivers:** policies, procedures, data systems
3. **Leadership Drivers:** technical, adaptive

Figure 5.3 The three drivers of implementation.

provide bus or gas vouchers, and it also gave the client an opportunity to build some rapport with the worker.

This is a pretty simple idea, right? Well, there was a lot of grumbling about it. Staff didn't feel they had time to do one more thing, and they were skeptical it would work. So, we decided, one small team of workers would give it a go as a sort of pilot. To make the results of our pilot a bit more obvious, we put a bulletin board up in the office to track the no-show rate for this team over time as compared to those who did not pilot this new intervention. We tracked the usual no-show rate for both groups of people, the intervention users, and those who didn't use the telephone intervention over a short period of time, like a couple of weeks maybe. It was like our own little quasi-experimental study. Then, we implemented the telephone intervention with the pilot team. Sure enough, we saw a clear decline in the no-show rate. It didn't bring the no-shows to zero, but it brought the rate down a lot and kept it down. The benefit was easier to see, and more believable, than just telling everyone that the intervention should work because it was "evidence-based."

NIRN, as a part of their Active Implementation Frameworks, has developed guidelines for usable innovations, implementation stages, implementation drivers, improvement cycles, and implementation teams. Detailed information on each of these aspects of the Active Implementation Framework is detailed on their website in a user-friendly hub (https://nirn.fpg.unc.edu/ai-hub). We will begin by describing the implementation drivers that help establish the capacity of a team, organization, or system to make the changes necessary to support successful implementation. These fall into three categories: competency drivers, organization drivers, and leadership drivers. Figure 5.3 lists these drivers.

Competency Drivers

These drivers are related to developing and sustaining the ability and confidence of the practitioners who will be using the new intervention. These are things like training, consultation, supervision, coaching, and evaluation. This also includes the basic skills, training, and competency of existing staff. Not all practitioners may be equally well suited to deliver all interventions, depending on things like experience, theoretical orientation, or "coach-ability." It makes a lot of sense to carefully consider these individual characteristics, as well as the current demands placed on a particular practitioner. For example, if someone has a very high caseload, they are not likely to be as successful in implementing a new intervention if they can barely keep up with the clients they are asked to serve. These competency drivers for ESI are mainly supported by training, coaching and consultation. Fidelity monitoring, or performance assessment, is used to make sure that these drivers are producing practices that indicate the ESI is being used correctly.

Organization Drivers

These drivers are those related to aligning administrative processes and practices to ensure that funding, policies, and procedures are in place to facilitate the use of the new intervention. These organizational drivers should be in place to ensure that the competency drivers are secured and maintained. So, organizational drivers should ensure that high-quality training is in place and that staff have the supports that they need to do the intervention accurately. This requires funding, as well as the protection of staff and administrative time to deliver adequate training and supervision, as well as processes to monitor the quality of the intervention and whether or not desired outcomes are being achieved. This includes examining fidelity and outcomes data. If it turns out that the intervention is not being done correctly, or the outcomes are not being achieved, these drivers can be adjusted to provide more supports.

In our experience working with many organizations, these drivers can be difficult to align with the implementation of a new intervention. A lot of social work organizations have a large array of programs, some of which they have developed themselves, some of which they have used for many years. It can take a lot of time an energy to re-examine and change these processes to appropriately support a new intervention, particularly a sophisticated ESI that requires much more investment in time and resources to be implemented correctly.

Leadership Drivers

NIRN highlights two types of leadership drivers that support implementation: technical and adaptive. Technical refers to leadership that is designed to solve fairly specific or straightforward challenges by putting into place generally well understood and accepted methods or processes. So, for example, let us say that an intervention is not working well at your agency and the problem seems to be inadequate space and consistent funding to support the intervention. The problem is pretty clear, and so is the solution—likely grant writing or fund-raising. However, some problems require work groups that identify and seek to understand what the problem is and then develop a consensus as to how to move forward toward a solution. This is adaptive leadership. For example, if your team discovers that the intervention is not producing outcomes as expected, this will take some further study and a team of individuals to sort out what is going on and formulate a solution.

While the implementation drivers help your agency to think about how to develop and support the infrastructure needed to successfully adopt and implement a new ESI, the stages of implementation help the implementation team prepare for their journey and know what to expect during the implementation process.

Stages of Implementation

Much like the EBP process, implementation is not a single step, but rather a process that can be described in stages that may overlap, and the process is never really complete, but rather circular in nature. Moving through each of the stages just once can take years. NIRN describes the five stages of implementation: exploration, installation, initial implementation, full implementation, and maintenance.

Exploration

Exploration is the stage in which practitioners assess the degree to which an intervention meets the needs of the organization or client and whether it's feasible. This requires gathering key stakeholders involved. Depending on the intervention under consideration, stakeholders might include administrators, clients, community leaders, policymakers, or others who will be tasked with using the intervention, paying for the services, or otherwise supporting the intervention.

For example, when one of us worked with a small social service agency in Saint Louis, Missouri, to examine the possibility of implementing a new intervention across their agency, we gathered together an implementation team, which included social workers who would use the intervention, the administrator who would ultimately budget for and approve the use of the intervention, students who would provide support for the intervention as interns, and trainers at the agency who would be responsible for getting new staff skilled up in the intervention once it was implemented in the agency. This implementation team will look different depending on the structure and nature of the agency or organization.

This is also the stage where different intervention possibilities are vetted. In the case of the St. Louis team, we constructed a table that allowed us to compare and summarize the different elements of each possible intervention. The implementation team may consider whether to implement a particular intervention or may be choosing from a variety of options. It is also important to examine the key elements of each intervention under consideration so that it is clear to the team what is needed to use the program correctly and anticipate any barriers that may get in the way. We have worked with social service agencies that have chosen an intervention based only on the strength of the research supporting the intervention's outcomes, only to find that the program is far too expensive to support several months later—after a lot of time, effort, and money has been invested to purchase manuals and send people to training. It pays off to take the time to really consider the pros and cons of different options. Figure 5.4 includes a list of discussion questions that can be used by practitioners or teams to assess interventions in the exploration stage. These questions expand on many of the considerations raised in Chapter 4 (this volume) related to selecting an ESI.

At the end of this stage, the team should make a decision about whether a new intervention should be implemented, and, if so, which intervention should be implemented. The work of the team should also provide a lot of information as to what barriers should be anticipated and addressed as well as what resources are needed to move the process forward.

Installation Stage

In this stage, the team works to gather all of the resources that are needed to implement the intervention. The work of the installation team should be driven by work of the implementation team in the evaluation stage. The members of the installation team may be the same or different than the evaluation team. Not only are the resources secured but barriers are also addressed, so different staff or consultant team members might be needed. For example, it might be particularly advantageous to involve clients or members of the community in the evaluation team, but they may not be as equipped to assist with internal resources. At this stage funding, training, staff, materials, and other resources are secured and aligned to support the intervention. At the end of this stage the implementation team has, to the best of its ability, done all the preparation necessary to begin using the new intervention.

Need:
1. What data do we have that informs this specific areas of need (administrative data, community needs assessments, client feedback, referral data), and what does these data tell us about this area of need?
2. What are the key outcomes that we want to address with the implementation of a new intervention?
3. Has the intervention been developed for clients that are similar to the ones we hope to serve?
4. Has the intervention been used in an agency or community similar to ours?

Fit:
5. How well does the intervention fit with other interventions that we are using? Is it complementary? Redundant?
6. How well does the intervention fit with the priorities of our organization?
7. How well does the intervention fit with the priorities of our funders, community, clients, or other stakeholders?

Resources:
8. Is the intervention manual or other supporting materials readily available? Where/how can they be obtained?
9. What is the cost of the manual and other supporting materials?
10. Do we have enough staff available to support the use of a new intervention?
11. Are local training and consultation resources available for the intervention? Evidence:
12. Does rigorous research evidence suggest that this intervention addresses these outcomes?
13. Does the intervention result in outcomes that are both statistically and clinically significant?
14. Has the intervention show effectiveness across a diverse array of clients, contexts, and outcomes?
15. Are there fidelity assessment instruments available?

Readiness:
16. Is there an "expert", technical assistance provider, or consultant who can help with the implementation process?
17. Has this intervention been used in the region or state with success?
18. Are the core elements of the intervention clearly defined by a manual, videos, or other resources?

Capacity:
19. Do we have the staff with the required skills and training to support the intervention? If not, can staff be hired or skilled up to the appropriate level?
20. Do we have the space, technology, and other resources needed to support the intervention?

Figure 5.4 Evaluation stage discussion questions for implementation teams.

Initial Implementation

In this stage, the work moves beyond planning and preparation. This is the point at which service providers make their initial attempt to deliver the intervention. The goal at the end of this stage of the work is to move the new intervention toward a place where it is considered "business as usual." The intervention should be integrated into the infrastructure and processes of the agency.

There can be a lot of anxiety, pushback, or unanticipated problems that might arise at this point in the process that derail the implementation effort. The tendency, in our experience, is for practices to slip back into whatever they were doing before implementing the new intervention. It is almost like a gravitational pull back to tradition. Of course, we have another story to tell you. One of us worked with a team of researchers on a study designed to examine the effect of a decision support tool for child welfare that was supposed to help workers make referrals for families to mental health services and also do some assessments that might help them screen for common problems experienced by children and families. This will date the project a bit—and some of you are not going to know what we're talking about at all—but this decision support tool was in the form of a Palm Pilot. This technology has been replaced by smartphones, but at the time these personal digital assistants (PDAs) were the pretty cutting-edge technology and did a lot: gave directions, accessed the Web, and organized your calendar. The idea was that this sort of PDA technology could replace all the paper notebooks and three-ring binders that child welfare workers often relied on to organize their referral information. The PDA could be much more easily shared across workers, updated frequently, and be connected to zip code data so you could see which referrals were most easily accessed by families in their area. The child welfare agency we worked with served some rural areas, so geography and distance were a particularly big deal.

This was a pretty simple intervention. It didn't take a lot of training, and in focus groups conducted at the start of the study, the workers all said that they liked the idea of the technology and would use it. So, what happened? At first, they did use it. But then, for most of them, their use trailed off. The more experienced workers slowly but surely wanted to ditch the PDAs with this nifty technology and go back to what they were used to: the three ring binders and paper notebooks. It was amazing how quickly this happened. Things really fell back to tradition within six months or so. The exceptions were the new workers. The two newest workers kept using the PDA. Our thinking was that the folks who were relatively new to the job hadn't become accustomed to using three-ring binders and notebooks, so the PDA technology was what they were trained in and thought of as the best way to make referrals and do screening around mental health. In this example, our implementation team did not do enough in the initial implementation stage to get the more seasoned workers over that hump.

At this stage implementation teams need to work hard to get everyone over that hump. Things like getting staff trained in their new roles vis-à-vis the intervention, making sure that administrative processes and procedures facilitate these new roles, and making sure that the implementation remains a "front burner" priority. Another thing that we have noticed over the years is that there is a lot of initial excitement over a new policy, practice, or intervention. But that excitement wears off over time and continually trying to use a new intervention becomes tiresome. If the new policy, practice, or intervention is no longer perceived as a priority, maybe because of new competing demands, the necessary time and energy needed to successfully move beyond this stage will not be invested, and the implementation will be derailed.

Full Implementation

The goal at the full implementation stage is to get the majority of folks in an organization using the new intervention, and doing so well and to good effect. According to NIRN, this means 50% or more of the practitioners, staff, or team members are using the intervention effectively with fidelity and good outcomes. At this point, the intervention is integrated into usual business. This does not mean that you are on easy street. There is still a need for the implementation team to continue to bring more people, processes, and procedures in line with the intervention as intended and troubleshooting to be done. Procedures and resources for training and coaching new staff as the organization experiences turnover need to be put in place. Booster trainings and ongoing clinical support, including processes for monitoring fidelity to the intervention are needed and should be planned, scheduled, and maintained for the long haul. There are a lot of threats to the maintenance of high-quality interventions: turnover, competing demands on time, and the introduction of other new interventions, policies, or procedures, among other things. If a long-term monitoring and maintenance plan is not in place, there is a good chance that drift back toward whatever practices were formerly in place will set in.

Box 5.2

If a long-term monitoring and maintenance plan is not in place, there is a good chance that drift back toward whatever practices were formerly in place will set in.

Using Interventions That Are Not ESI

In many cases you might find that you plan to provide an intervention that is not an ESI and doesn't have all the components in place to support implementation. Or you may even be working from scratch to develop and support your own intervention. Regardless, these tools and processes can be used to make sure that you or your staff are implementing your chosen intervention as you intend and continue to do so over time. Evidence-supported or not, there is a tendency for policies, programs, and practices to drift over time—or to fail to be implemented with a high degree of quality to begin with. Practitioners are well-advised to think through the supports that are needed to implement and maintain high-quality services.

Example: Implementing Evidence-Based Child Welfare: The New York City Experience

This example was generously shared by Dr. Allison Metz, director of NIRN, based on work she has recently done in partnership with the New York City Administration for Children's Services (ACS) and Casey Family Programs (Clara, Garcia, & Metz, 2017; Metz & Bartley, 2015). In 2011, New York's ACS and Casey Family Programs partnered to provide 11 empirically supported practice models in its continuum of preventative care with the goals of improving family functioning and child well-being, reducing repeat maltreatment and preventing placement in foster care (Clara et al., 2017). Early in the process, ACS invited NIRN to partner and provide guidance in utilizing implementation science as a framework for the initiative and the training of staff and collaborating agencies. The core guiding principle of NIRN is that implementation is a developmental process that occurs in stages—exploration, installation, initial implementation, and full implementation. This process is not always linear and may be messy, overlapping, and revisit earlier stages as needed. Conceptually, success is viewed as needing an effective innovation (ESI), effective implementation, and an enabling context to lead to socially significant outcomes (Clara et al., 2017). From here on out we describe the implementation process as implemented via these stages with ACS per the materials provided by Dr. Metz and her team.

Exploration

The first step—exploration—was obviously complex when selecting ESIs for as large of a population as New York ACS serves. This process began with ACS determining which ESIs would be most appropriate for their population and goals, beginning with those already being used. The populations considered included families with young children, families with teens, and families who had recently indicated or substantiated cases of physical abuse or neglect. The targeted needs that were prioritized included trauma-informed models, behavior-focused models, and family therapy models. The 11 selected ESIs were then categorized across the ACS preventative service continuum by level of risk and service need. Some examples of these ESIs included Functional Family Therapy for Child Welfare, Brief Strategic Family Therapy, and Trauma Systems Therapy. During this initial step, an accountable structure or implementation team was also initiated to support exploration activities and in the development of communication protocols. While the team changed slightly over time, it remained active and cohesive throughout all stages of implementation. In addition, to increase partnership with the provider community, ACS sponsored open houses to introduce both the ESIs and the implementation science approach and plan. Finally, NIRN conducted a "listening tour" with ACS staff and providers during this initial stage to assess staff and provider perspectives regarding the strengths and challenges of implementing ESIs within ACS. The results from this listening tour were used to support communication and build readiness with ACS staff and providers to inform the installation stage.

Installation

The installation stage is focused on securing and developing support structures and tools needed to install the ESI, which can include "communication protocols, financial and human resources, and even internal enthusiasm for the initiative (Clara et al., 2017, p. 13). Feedback loops between frontline practitioners and administration are particularly important so that challenges can be addressed as they emerge. To support this process, agencies contracting to provide services were given options and time to establish new contracts to provide one or more of the ESIs. In addition, ACS set up an Implementation Institute for staff to learn about implementation science, ESI developers presented on their models to ACS staff, NIRN and ACS created learning modules based on findings of the drivers analysis (which assessed what would be needed with regard to leadership, competency, and organizational infrastructure to provide the ESIs), and assigned program development managers to each ESI so that providers and developers would have a consistent point of contact at ACS. These program development managers have consistently coordinated ongoing communication between providers and model developers on a biweekly basis, as well as monthly calls with each.

Initial and Full Implementation

After four years, the project was in the initial implementation stage after key milestones of establishing expression of interest (EOI) contracts and request for proposal (RFP) contracts within the first year. During this time, ACS gathered data to monitor implementation progress and improvement strategies based on this data. With changes in ACS administration, the agency has increased its commitment to ESIs as the process has progressed, with efforts to increase the size of some programs and interest in exploring more sustainable methods to track program fidelity and enthusiasm regarding the implementation science approach in both child welfare and more broadly among public officials. For this project to achieve full implementation the ESIs will need to be fully stabilized with at least half of practitioners implementing the ESIs with fidelity as evidenced through data collection. There has progress in getting to this point, however, as ACS is doing the work of full implementation with regard to "highly functioning improvement cycles," whereby there is bidirectional forms of communication between policy and practice facilitated by the teams. These efforts will ideally lead to additional supports to sustain the ESIs. It is not uncommon, especially within such a large organization with multiple ESIs, for a program to take at least two to four years to gain full implementation of a new practice. One important lesson learned by both providers and developers is that successful and sustainable implementation takes time and commitment (Clara et al., 2017).

Sustainability

Clara et al. (2017) emphasize that sustainability should be a major focus form the beginning of the implementation process. In this case, ACS developed a Sustaining and Integrating Preventative EBMs (SIPE) team, which consisted of cross-divisional leadership with goals to expand commitment and leadership of ESIs across ACS diversion, provide an accountable structure to support and sustain ESIs, and continue to address system barriers to sustainable implementation of these models. They have achieved these aims primarily by increasing knowledge through case presentations, solving problems by identifying challenges and bringing the key players to the table to develop solutions, and using targeted, short-term workshops to develop tools or propose improvements to the current system (e.g., a frequently asked questions document; Clara et al., 2017).

Current Observable Impact

Casey Family Programs conducted individual and small group interviews with select ACS staff, providers, developers. and families to get a better sense of how the ACS system has changed (Clara et al., 2017). Overall, interviewees reported

- Higher levels of knowledge and internal ACS expertise with regard to ESIs and increased buy-in to the ESIs across ACS divisions;
- Strong collaboration between ACS, ESI developers, and provider agencies;
- Modifications to the Preventative Scorecard, ACS's performance evaluation tool, increasing alignment between ACS's standards and ESI fidelity measures;
- Modifications to the preventative services referral process, including the development of a new instrument for referral; and
- Increased understanding and application of implementation science.

With regard to program outcomes, New York City now provides ESIs to 25% of families compared to 4% prior to 2013 (Clara et al., 2017). Preliminary outcomes also indicate ACS has increased its capacity to serve families due to a shorter length of service with adopted ESIs, with an average of 1.2 families seen per paid slot from 0.95 before prior to the project. Also, there are a higher proportion of closed cases in high-risk program models, an increased collaboration via joint collaboration meetings between ACS's Divisions of Child Protection and preventative providers, lower proportions of indicated investigations for families receiving ESIs compared to general services, and a decrease in the number of indicated investigations within six months of finishing preventative services (Clara et al., 2017). Finally, parents interviewed shared feeling very supported by their ESI practitioner and were able to state specific ways in which there has been positive change in their families' lives.

Challenges

While there are some emerging successes of this large effort, there were also challenges and lessons learned. The biggest challenge identified was the turnover of staff providing ESIs at provider agencies. The reasons for turnover included competing with higher salaries offered by other sectors and the intense nature of the work. With turnover, training and funding of training became a challenge as well. While ACS initially factored in training and developer costs, it was not enough to cover all costs with higher than anticipated turnover, and this created a significant cost burden for some providers. One way to address these challenges was for agencies providing the same intervention to share training materials and partner in training their staff. Also, despite many efforts to ensure communication worked consistently, there were still some challenges in properly referring families for ESIs and across ACS and New York more broadly to ensure buy-in and support. A final challenge has been how to monitor fidelity of all ESIs in the ACS system, with each fidelity assessment looking quite different across ESIs. The lack of consistency across programs, as well as varied indicators and rubrics made it difficult to figure out how to accommodate these fidelity measures within their existing data systems. Going forward, one goal is to develop a "common currency" among fidelity measures to better support and sustain fidelity in child welfare systems. For further reading and examples, Metz et al. (2015) also discuss the application of active implementation frameworks in another child welfare context, whereby high-fidelity was established.

Discussion Questions

1. What is the difference between diffusion, dissemination, adoption, and implementation? How are they related?
2. How important is it to have models to guide the implementation of ESIs? How might they help? What barriers might there be to making them work in organizational settings?
3. What accounts for the tendency for policies, programs, and practices to drift away from their original design? What characteristics of organizations or practitioners make drift more or less likely?
4. What strategies could be used to make social workers more comfortable with observation of their practice with clients, whether through audio, video, or in-person?
5. How do each of the implementation drivers relate to one another? For example, how do competency drivers have an impact on leadership and organizational drivers and vice versa?

6

Adaptation and the Internal Logic of Interventions

In this chapter, we'll talk about both adaptation and the internal logic of interventions, because you need to think carefully about how interventions work—or are supposed to work—in practice, before you can understand how to change them to improve their fit or benefit to the clients and communities with whom you work. Also, understanding the internal logic of an intervention is also essential to crafting fidelity strategies that are designed to make sure interventions are delivered and maintained as they were intended.

Adaptation is challenging to define. But defining adaptation is an important place to start—mainly because there is a lot of disagreement about how and when to do adaptation work, as well as who should be allowed to adapt interventions. The adaptation concepts we are going to review here are strewn across a variety of disciplines and areas of study. These different bodies of work rarely "talk with one another." Which means everyone is coming up with their own ideas about adaptation and calling it different things.

For example, some adaptation researchers have been working hard on cultural adaptation (e.g., Castro, Berrera, & Martinez, 2004). They are focused on learning how existing interventions might be changed or improved to better serve cultural groups that are different from the group for whom an intervention was originally developed or tested. For example, very few interventions have been developed for or with American Indian (AI) youth and their families. It may be that the unique cultural context of AI youth and their families would mean that interventions developed for, say, Caribbean Black youth and their families may not work as well or may be rejected by the AI community.

Other adaptation researchers, many of whom are in public health, have been focused on adaptations to health communications (e.g., Kreuter & Skinner, 2000). Rather than focusing on cultural adaptation, these folks have been thinking about how to craft messages about health-related behaviors to different people who vary by a variety of characteristics such as race, gender, age, or medical condition in a way that maximizes the likelihood they will benefit from the health messages delivered to them. For example, research suggests that the reasons male and female college students are motivated to drink alcohol are different (e.g., Tyler, Schmitz, & Adams, 2017). So the messages aimed at reducing campus drinking among undergraduate men might need to be different than the messages aimed at undergraduate women. There are a lot of other examples of adaptation work, some of which are very complex and require the consideration of multiple intersecting client characteristics and identities, all of which could impact how well interventions work. Adapting interventions previously designed for middle class white mothers to serve low-income fathers of color, for example, requires thinking through the role of gender and culture.

Sometimes adaptations are needed, not because of client characteristics, but rather due to other practical differences. For example, other researchers and practitioners have made changes to interventions to better suit different contexts of practice—say, moving a mental health intervention that was developed for use in clinics into schools. Others have adapted interventions to deal with different constraints of practice, such as limitations in resources or time. Many, many, people have tried to make interventions briefer, cheaper, or more easily delivered by folks without expensive clinical training.

What Is Adaptation?

Given that there isn't really a cohesive set of ideas and definitions around adaptation, we will lay out what we see as some of the most important terms and concepts for practitioners to think about as they consider adapting interventions in general and ESI in particular.

We think of *adaptation* as a broad umbrella term used to describe a lot of different possible changes to interventions, made by different people for different reasons. Others have defined the term *adaptation* in ways that reflect some of their beliefs about what exactly about an intervention can be adapted and by whom. For example, in their writing on cultural adaptation of prevention interventions, Castro, Barrera, and Martinez (2004) describe program adaptation as "the modification of program content to accommodate the needs of a specific consumer group" (p. 41). Because their work is focused on a particular characteristic of clients, their culture, their definition focuses on adaptations to address the mismatch between the clients and the interventions but does not address the service context within which the program is used.

Another broad definition has been provided by Backer (2001) in a report on fidelity and adaptation of substance abuse prevention programs. In this report, adaptation was defined as "deliberate or accidental modification" of a program,

---

Box 6.1

Drift is what happens when safeguards are not in place to protect the quality and integrity of a practice, intervention, program, or policy.

---

including deletions and additions, modification of the nature of components, and changes in the manner or intensity of a program, as well as any cultural modifications (p. 7). Although a strength of Backer's definition is that it is broad and not limited to changes to address the mismatch between clients and interventions alone, we would not include "accidental modifications" under adaptation. These accidental types of changes to interventions are better described as *drift*. As we discussed in Chapter 5 (this volume), drift is what happens when safeguards are not in place to protect the quality and integrity of a practice, intervention, program, or policy. Drift may occur due to a lack of supervision, poor training, staff turnover, or other processes that threaten the quality of the implementation. This is, we argue, a process distinct from purposeful modifications made to interventions in response to the needs of clients and service contexts.

Not everyone has adopted such a broad view of adaptation. Others have specified adaptation in terms of who makes the changes, for example, distinguishing between changes made by intervention or program developers versus changes made by the users of interventions and programs. Some folks feel that only those who have developed an intervention have the authority or knowledge of the intervention needed to properly adapt an intervention. A tremendous amount of time, thought, and research has gone into the development of interventions and programs, particularly those that have been established as ESI. This is a valid concern, and it is fair to say that intervention developers may be best equipped to adapt their interventions; however, intervention developers do not likely have the time to invest in making adaptations to their interventions to suit every client group and every potential service context in which the intervention might be used.

Internal Logic of Interventions

Others have limited their view of adaptation to changes that do not contradict the "internal logic" of an intervention (e.g., Harshbarger, Simmons, Coelho, Sloop, & Collins, 2006). In other words, anyone can make changes, as long as the essence of an intervention is unchanged. Counter to this perspective, we choose to include adaptations that may compromise the internal logic of interventions for a few reasons. First, efficacy research on many interventions lacks empirical data validating the internal logic of an intervention. It is often unclear which elements and mechanisms are critical to the success of an intervention. The way interventions work, or why, is mostly a black box. For example, a lot of evidence-supported anxiety interventions have some component aimed at helping clients learn relaxation techniques. We don't know, however, what would happen if we took that part out of an anxiety treatment. We might hypothesize the intervention would not work as well, but, in truth, we probably don't know for sure. Or, if it does contribute to the outcome, by how much does it contribute? Maybe we could remove it to try and save some time and in turn lose a little impact, but maybe that is OK if we are making a purposeful tradeoff. Or, perhaps relaxation is the *only* component that really matters very much in anxiety treatments, and the rest of it—cognitive work, biofeedback, desensitization—doesn't really contribute much more above and beyond simply learning some really good relaxation approaches and practicing them.

There are even more nuanced questions about the internal logic of intervention and programs like: "Does it matter if we focus on relaxation first, or can we do relaxation work later in the intervention just as well?" "Does it matter for how long we focus on relaxation; will spending more time on that component make the intervention work better?" "What if we teach relaxation through breathing-oriented techniques versus something else, does it matter?" These are questions related not only to the identifying of the working logic, or critical components of the intervention, but also dosage, methods, and ordering effects.

Although ESIs are usually based on sound theory and efficacy trials, the effect of the intervention is most often estimated together as a package and the effectiveness of the intervention is demonstrated at the group level. Usually rigorous studies test whether the whole intervention, as specified by the manual, works or does not work. There are relatively few dismantling studies, or studies that break interventions down into their parts. These dismantling studies are the ones designed to demonstrate the degree to which different intervention elements actually contribute to the treatment effect and begin to parse out the relative contribution of different elements, dosage, and ordering effects. Existing efforts to analyze the core elements of interventions, sometimes referred to as *core components analysis*, are most often based on theoretical, not empirical, analyses (Backer, 2001). We also lack studies that test moderators that may help explain variation in treatment effects across individuals. So, while a computer-based social isolation intervention may work very well for older clients as a group, it may not work well for those that have cognitive deficits that impact their ability to navigate the online environment. In this example, cognitive ability is a moderating factor. Moderators may not change how an intervention works, but rather how well it works for clients with certain characteristics.

Research on the Impact of Adaptations

Interventions are arguably more than the sum of their parts and making changes to the elements and mechanisms hypothesized to be critical to their efficacy could fundamentally harm the integrity of the intervention or program. However, emerging research on the core elements of interventions for children and adolescents suggests that practitioners can, with some structure and guidance, make decisions about which intervention elements to offer to which clients and make changes to ordering and dosage of intervention elements to good effect (Weisz et al., 2012). Kaminski, Valle, Filene, and Boyle (2008) also failed to find evidence that use of a traditional manual itself had any impact on parent training effect sizes and hypothesized instead that it is the use of effective interventions elements, regardless of manualization, that boosts outcomes. These studies suggest that the precise collection of intervention elements, dosage, and ordering indicated by intervention packages may be less important than once thought and that a relatively greater degree of flexibility in adapting interventions may result in improved outcomes and access to higher-quality services for clients.

In some instances it may be reasonable to remove a component of an intervention, even if it will likely reduce the overall effect of the intervention, so that it may be more broadly disseminated in practice (e.g., the intervention may be more affordable or more acceptable to clients if shortened). For example, we have worked with a number of social service agencies who have rejected interventions simply because they are too time-consuming. Unfortunately, the empirical data to make these type of reasonable tradeoffs are largely absent so it is tough to make these nuanced decisions using research evidence.

Here we use the term *adaptation* as a broadly inclusive term, but we do emphasize that adaptation should specifically include *purposeful* changes to intervention content, context, and methods in response to the needs of diverse client groups or service contexts, regardless of who implements the change or the components of the intervention that are changed. Purposeful efforts to adapt interventions, regardless of the methods or quality of the process and results, signal unmet needs or concerns of service providers or clients. There is value in attending to the factors that motivate service providers to engage in adaptation and that service providers as well as clients can provide important insights into the limitations of current ESI.

Targeting and Tailoring

Under the umbrella of adaptation, there are additional useful ideas that speak to different approaches to making changes to interventions. Borrowing from

> ### Box 6.2
>
> Here we use the term *adaptation* as a broadly inclusive term, but we do emphasize that adaptation should specifically include *purposeful* changes to intervention content, context, and methods in response to the needs of diverse client groups or service contexts, regardless of who implements the change or the components of the intervention that are changed.

the field of health communication, adapting an intervention to fit the needs of a particular subgroup of clients is referred to as *targeting*. Targeting an intervention or service for a defined subgroup of clients is a form of adaptation that takes into account characteristics shared by the subgroup's members (Kreuter & Skinner, 2000). Adapting parent training programs for subgroups of parents including Mexican American parents, foster parents, or fathers, for example, are all examples of targeting.

Tailoring, by contrast, refers to adaptation that is intended to address variation at the individual client level. Kreuter and Skinner (2000) define tailoring as "any combination of information or change strategies intended to reach one specific person, based on characteristics that are unique to that person, related to the outcome of interest, and have been derived from an individual assessment" (p. 1). Although the discussion of tailoring has often focused on individual characteristics, tailoring has also been applied to address the unique characteristics of a specific family as well, whereby the assessment information would take into account the characteristics of the family as a system. Similarly, at the macro level, an intervention might be tailored to a particular neighborhood, city, or state based on its individual characteristics. For example, in child welfare, some state child welfare systems are largely administered at the state level, while others are run through counties. Some child welfare systems serve primarily urban areas, while others include a mix of rural and urban communities. Other systems have large immigrant or refugee populations, while others don't. So child welfare interventions might need to be tailored to address unique collection of system characteristics such as whether the system is state- or county-led system and urban, rural, or mixed, as well as the size of the immigrant or refugee population.

The key to distinguishing targeting from tailoring is whether the adaptation is designed to address a group that includes multiple individuals, couples, families, or other targeted clients as a subgroup with shared characteristics, or a single individual, couple, family, or other identified client with unique characteristics. For example, a parent training intervention may be targeted for adolescent fathers, or it may be tailored to the particular needs of one particular adolescent father. There are a lot of different individual client characteristics that might warrant some amount of tailoring. For example, the use of information about an individual's current level of readiness to change figures prominently in the existing health communications literature, but other individual characteristics such as age, cultural preferences, and community context have also been used to individually tailor health communications as well.

Clinical Tailoring

Practitioners regularly engage in tailoring where clinical judgment and experience are used to make adjustments to treatments based on individual characteristics (Zayas, Bellamy, & Proctor, 2012). This is sometimes referred to as *clinical tailoring*. Scholarship on the concept of cultural competence has described the efforts of clinicians to make adjustments to interventions based on their knowledge of clients' cultural perspectives, individual preferences, or other characteristics—this practice is clinical tailoring. Some of the challenges identified in that literature include professionals' lack of familiarity, comfort, or experience serving racial or ethnic minority groups and the underrepresentation of racial and ethnic minority groups among practitioners.

This concept can be extended to apply to working with other underserved groups, such as fathers. For example, men are not well represented in the profession of social work, and studies have highlighted parenting intervention social service providers' lack of comfort, or even fear of, working with men. Service providers could be trained to be more father-friendly, or competent, in clinically tailoring interventions for male clients on an as-needed basis.

Peripheral and Core Elements

Peripheral Elements

Oftentimes targeting is discussed as the domain of intervention developers and researchers, whereas tailoring is the domain of clinicians. To this end, tailoring is frequently limited to adapting ESI around the margins in ways that do not compromise the integrity, or the internal logic, of the intervention. These elements are described by some as *peripheral elements*. Examples of peripheral intervention elements include language and images. For example, an intervention may be translated from English to Spanish, and examples used to illustrate skills might be changed to reflect culturally relevant stories or scenarios. Translating an intervention from one language to another is not likely to impact its internal logic. The same material, the same handouts, and the same procedures are used—they are just used in a different language.

Some intervention manuals now include information about what can and cannot be changed by practitioners or suggest possible adaptations. In this book, we have used Dads Matter-HV, an intervention designed to engage fathers in home visiting, as an example. Dads Matter-HV includes suggested adaptations for delivering intervention content in person or over the phone, as well as with mothers and fathers together in conjoint sessions or on their own in individual sessions. Home visitors can provide the intervention elements in different orders and can skip over content depending on the needs of the families they work with. These changes don't fundamentally change the clinical content of the home visiting intervention, they change the way the intervention is delivered.

Core Elements

Peripheral intervention elements stand in contrast to what we will refer to as *core elements* of an intervention. The concept of core elements, the clinical elements of an intervention that fundamentally define the nature of a program (Backer, 2001), has been widely described in the adaptation literature. Other terms have been used to describe similar concepts such as key ingredients, core components, and mechanisms of change. You may decide to adapt the core elements of an intervention, and there are some very good reasons to do so as we'll discuss in the next chapter.

Some of the core elements of Dads Matter-HV include teaching parents to set goals, problem-solve, and set roles and expectations together with the child's other parent. All of these core elements are designed to be delivered in the first four months of services. These are delivered to mothers and fathers in sessions through methods that include asking parents specific questions, raising discussion points, information-giving, and exercises. These core elements are integrated into the intervention because our research team believes, based on theory and prior research, that these elements are essential to building a strong co-parenting relationship. If one of these core elements were removed, our research team would likely feel that the intervention no longer has the same integrity or power to impact the outcomes we are aiming to improve.

Other core elements, however, might include values or principles that are included in the intervention. For example, in Dads Matter-HV, the manual directs home visitors to include fathers as equal parenting partners with mothers in the home-visiting intervention from the beginning of services and continually work to engage them directly and in person, if possible. Again, based on theory and prior studies, we believe that it is less successful to try and engage fathers later in services after mothers have been engaged. If the home visitor only engages mom to begin with, then the implicit messages to fathers and mothers is that dad is less important and that the service is for moms not dads. In addition, we have found that because fathers are less accustomed to participating in parenting services and may face more barriers to participation, they must be continuously and explicitly engaged. If these practice principles are not incorporated, then our research team would say that the internal logic of the intervention is compromised.

Different interventions have different core and peripheral elements, although some "families" of intervention likely have many of these elements in common. For example, Table 6.1 provides a list of core versus peripheral elements common to parent training interventions based on a meta-analysis of the research on these interventions (Kaminski et al., 2008).

In some cases, core and peripheral elements are clearly outlined by intervention developers and explicitly described in the intervention manual, including information about whether and, if so, how core and peripheral elements may be changed. In other cases, this is less clear. Sometimes you can find general

Table 6.1 **Examples of Core and Peripheral Elements of Parent Training Interventions**

Core Elements Include Teaching Parents . . .	*Peripheral Elements Include . . .*
Child development knowledge and care	Providing services individually or in a group
Positive interactions with child	Language translation
Responsiveness, sensitivity and nurturing	Using videos versus verbal examples to illustrate techniques
Emotional communication	
Disciplinary communication	Including couples versus single parents
Positive reinforcement	Providing food, transportation, or childcare
Use of time-outs	Conducting services in a clinic, school, or church
Problem-solving	
Consistent responding	
Promoting children's social skills	
Promoting children's cognitive/academic skills	

Adapted from J. W. Kaminski, L. A. Valle, J. H. Filene, & C. L. Boyle, 2008, A meta-analytic review of components associated with parent training program effectiveness. *Journal of Abnormal Child Psychology,* 36, 567–589.

outlines of core and peripheral elements for families of interventions, as in the example of parent training interventions.

In general, core elements should be adapted with more caution than peripheral elements. It's not that peripheral elements are unimportant. Peripheral elements too can have a big impact on the intervention's success. For example, although parent training is not defined by whether transportation is provided, if you are delivering parent training in a rural area where public transportation is hard to come by, providing rides to your clients may make the all the difference in participation. No matter how solid the intervention is, if people don't come, they won't benefit from it.

Common Factors

Other research suggests *common factors*, or factors that are broadly reflected in successful interventions regardless of model or theoretical orientation, account for the lion's share of intervention outcomes. So, instead of placing so much emphasis on core and peripheral elements, common factors acknowledges the role of the clinical content, values, and techniques included in an intervention, but underscores the importance of other factors.

For example, Asay and Lambert (2008) reviewed the literature on common factors of interventions and suggest that *clinical techniques* account for only a small portion of change related to interventions. Yet, clinical techniques are often the central focus of discussions about EBP. Other common factors include extratherapeutic factors, expectancy, and the therapeutic relationship—all of which have been associated with outcomes in research studies regardless of the specific intervention elements used. Figure 6.1 presents the common factors, including the estimated amount of change in outcomes contributed by each factor.

Extratherapeutic factors are part of the client or the clients' environment. These factors might include characteristics such as motivation or intelligence, as well things like family, friends, and community supports. *Expectancy* is the client's knowledge that they are receiving treatment and have some expectation for improvement. When people buy-in to an intervention, they are more likely to benefit from it. This is analogous to a placebo effect in intervention studies. The *therapeutic relationship* is the fourth factor and includes the client's perception of their therapist as warm, empathic, and accepting as well as the agreement between the client and the practitioner on the tasks and goals of treatment.

The common factors framework can help broaden the lens of adaptation beyond changes to core and peripheral elements, or techniques included in interventions, alone. The common factors framework can be used to organize and test adaptations for specific intervention/client adaptation problems across

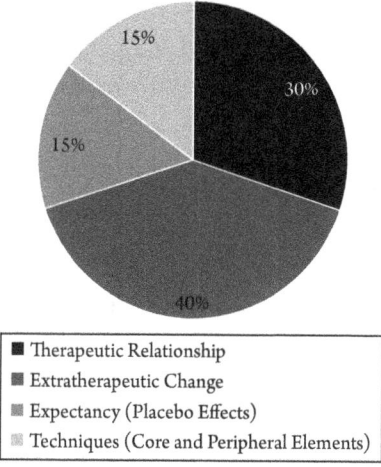

Figure 6.1 The common factors. *Source*: Reproduced from T. P. Asay & M. J. Lambert, 2008, The empirical case for the common factors in therapy: Quantitative findings. In M. A. Hubble, B. L. Duncan, & S. D. Miller (Eds.), *The heart and soul of change: What works in therapy* (pp. 23–55). Washington, DC: American Psychological Association.

interventions/client groups and may generate more opportunities for the integration of findings different adaptation efforts. For example, what is the relative impact of adaptations that target relational factors? If our goal is to increase fathers' engagement in home-visiting interventions, what would be the effect of developing general father-friendliness training for home visitors? In fact, in our research, we have found that some of the barriers to fathers' engagement in child and family interventions seems to be related to the attitudes and beliefs of the practitioners. So, we might try to improve clinicians' father-friendliness and see if these improvements result in better outcomes across a variety of parenting interventions such as parent training and home visiting. Or, we could also target adaptations that change expectancy factors. For example, what if we implemented motivational interviewing techniques to increase fathers' and mothers' buy-in to the idea of fathers' participation in parenting services? Might this again increase fathers' engagement in, and benefit from, a variety of child and family services like home visiting without necessarily changing the core and peripheral elements of the intervention itself?

Challenges to the Adaptation Field

Adaptation work is challenging and complex. We need to think carefully about when to use targeting versus tailoring, or maybe forgo adaptation all together. In the next chapter we present some steps to figuring out whether you might have an adaptation that needs to be solved and, if so, what information you can use to determine what should be adapted to improve outcomes for clients.

Discussion Questions

1. What are the costs and benefits of practitioners making adaptations to interventions as compared to intervention developers making adaptations to interventions?
2. What are some of the factors that are likely to contribute to drift of an intervention?
3. What are the potential challenges and benefits of adapting the core and peripheral elements of an intervention versus making adaptations that target the other common factors (e.g., therapeutic relationship, extratherapeutic change, or expectancy)?

7

Identifying and Defining
an Adaptation Problem

Now that you know what adaptation is, and we are on the same page on the general terminology related to the elements of an intervention, the next question is whether to adapt an intervention. There isn't always a need for a formal adaptation effort. Sometimes clinical tailoring, or those small tweaks that practitioners make in their approach with each client, is all that is needed to address the unique client or context within which one is working. In some cases, clinical tailoring is not enough. How do you know?

To Adapt or Not to Adapt?

In this chapter we will walk you through the process of deciding whether there is an adaptation problem for you to solve. We will use an example from our work on adapting parent training to better serve fathers to illustrate how the adaptation concepts we described in Chapter 6 (this volume) might be applied to this particular problem.

Adaptation is difficult. If you are going to make the effort to purposefully and systematically change an intervention, there should be evidence of a concern about the way an intervention is working for clients or within the service context. We find it helpful to think of adaptation as a response to a mismatch between clients, interventions, and service contexts. Figure 7.1 depicts the potential for mismatch across clients, interventions, and service contexts with some examples of each type of mismatch to illustrate.

There are many cases where the fit between clients and interventions or service contexts and interventions is not strong. Clients may perceive the intervention as not being for them. For example, one of us recently had a conversation with a colleague who works in a state child welfare system about problem drinking among new, particularly young, parents. If you are a parent, you know

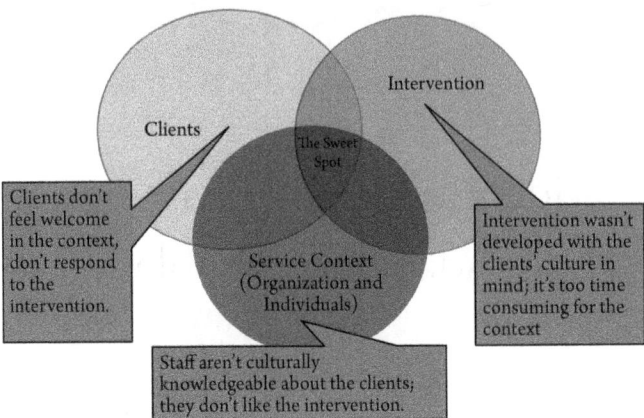

Figure 7.1 The client, intervention, and service context adaptation problems.

that parenting can be stressful. Possibly because of this stress, some new parents might use alcohol to relax or cope with the stress. They may drink while they are taking care of their children to an extent that they are not watching their children carefully, and children may be at an increased risk for things like accidents. In her opinion, the current interventions designed for problem drinking do not well address the needs of young parents who do not identify with services for people with alcohol problems, alcohol abuse, or addiction. So, they may not seek these services or actively resist them. Yet, their alcohol use may require intervention—and perhaps they might even benefit from some component of existing interventions aimed at reducing risky or harmful alcohol use. This is a mismatch between the intervention and the clients. Interventions aimed at problem alcohol use also may not be well suited for delivery in places where young parents are most likely to access supports—perhaps libraries or daycare centers. One of us recently did some focus groups with young rural parents about the community services that they find most helpful, and one of the most common responses were libraries. Interventions aimed at problem drinking are not commonly found in libraries. But could they be? Perhaps so, with a bit of adaptation. The mismatch between clients, interventions, and service contexts may be very great or quite small.

Identifying an Adaptation Problem

On occasion, an intervention can be so obviously mismatched to a group of clients or a particular service context that the need to adapt the intervention in particular ways seems obvious. For example, an intervention might be developed for use in a different language. The content of the intervention may need to be translated and back translated for accuracy and cultural congruence. Maybe that's all that's needed. Oftentimes, however, the adaptation problem is more complicated.

In those more complicated cases, evidence of an intervention's failure to serve a subgroup of clients, or failure to work in a particular context, should be identified before an evidence-supported intervention (ESI) is adapted for that group. Just so, adaptation is not always the answer. It may be a better option to identify an alternative intervention that has been built and evaluated for the population or context in which you are working. In other cases, it may be a better option to develop your own intervention, perhaps borrowing components from existing interventions. None of these approaches is easy, and depending on the situation, more than one option may be viable. Adapting an intervention, even in simple ways, is difficult work, and once you futz with an intervention, there is a very real risk that the core elements or key ingredients that made the intervention work in the first place could be compromised. So, the decision whether proceed along the adaptation process takes careful consideration.

Articulating the adaptation problem justifies the resources needed to engage in the adaptation process, provides some insight as to how the ESI might be adapted, and identifies where improvements in adaptation outcomes would be expected if adaptations are indeed successful. Take our example above with young parents with problem alcohol use. If we have evidence that this subgroup of the population simply is not participating in services and if we make changes to the intervention, we should see rates of participation go up. If we make adaptations for these young parents and their participation does not increase, we likely have not found the right solution to the adaptation problem.

Looking for evidence related to the mismatch between client, intervention, and service context also distinguishes adaptation problems from implementation problems, such as poor dissemination or implementation supports for the intervention. For example, an intervention that targets young parents' problem alcohol use may not be implemented very well in services because service providers were not adequately trained or do not have good enough supervision and feedback supports to maintain the intervention at a high level of quality. These are implementation problems, not problems with the intervention themselves. If this is the issue, then more attention to the implementation drivers described in Chapter 5 (this volume) is needed.

There are a number places where evidence might be available to point to a particular adaptation problem. These may be evidenced by clients, communities, or service contexts in things like poor participation. Successful adaptation is, in turn, evidenced by improvements in one or more of these areas. Again, if there is an adaptation problem related to clients' participation in the intervention as evidenced by poor rates of attendance, and the intervention is adapted to improve attendance, then attendance should be monitored before, during, and after the adaptation is made to figure out whether the adaptations were made as intended and the changes made to the intervention actually result in the expected improvements. This is yet another example of why organizational drivers described in Chapter 5 (this volume) should include the monitoring of both implementation of interventions, including adapted interventions, as well as outcomes.

Also, keep in mind that likely adaptations could be made to improve uptake and acceptance, response to intervention, or feasibility and sustainability of interventions. The question is one of priorities and the tradeoffs between effort and benefit. This is another place where it makes a lot of sense to work with colleagues as a team to identify which adaptation problems should be addressed and which ones should be addressed first.

Before we move on, just a couple of things to note here. First, there may be other conditions or situations that point to the need to adapt an intervention. For example, a particular group of clients may advocate for adaptations based on values, goals or expectations. If you are working in an area where the community is taking a strong role in crafting and guiding services, this may very well be the case. It's also important to note that although clients may not initially push for adaptations to ESI, their input is important to the process and is included in the next chapter as part of the adaptation process.

Although other conditions or situations may point to the need to adapt, these conditions were selected as they may be used to track whether the adaptation has worked, and they accommodate a broad range of adaptation problems. An adaptation problem may be evidenced across all three categories. However, other adaptation problems may suggest the need only to target one or two categories. Later we will use the example of the misalignment between existing models of parent training and the service needs of fathers as a case study of an adaptation problem to illustrate these points.

Evidence of Adaptation Problems for Clients

Table 7.1 provides some examples of evidence that suggest that you might have an adaptation problem among client subgroups or in your service context.

Table 7.1 **Evidence of the Need to Adapt**

Among Client Subgroups			In the Service Context
Participation	*Engagement*	*Efficacy*	*Feasibility and Sustainability*
Clients do not participate or participate in small numbers.	The quality of client engagement is poor (little participation, homework is not completed etc.).	Improvement or achievement of goals is very slow.	Staff do not have the skill or training necessary to master the intervention.
Dropout is high, or completion rates are low.		Only a small percentage of clients improve.	There isn't enough time available to complete the intervention.
		Improvements are not maintained over time.	The physical space needed to conduct the intervention is inadequate.
			Staff reject the intervention or do not buy into it.

Participation

Evidence of a misalignment between the intervention and client subgroup include low rates of intervention participation in comparison to other clients in general. Participation is challenging in many service contexts, so it is helpful to know whether the rate of participation you are observing is low within that context. For example, do you see differences between different client subgroups within your organization? If you notice that you have higher no-show rates among queer clients, this may point to an adaptation problem that may signal a poor fit between queer clients and your services. Participation problems might be signaled by poor recruitment or early drop out, or other evidence may suggest that a particular subgroup of clients might be relatively reluctant to begin or maintain participation in services. When we say "subgroup," we mean either your clients in general, or possibly a subgroup of your clients. So, you may serve the same community as other social service agencies. Do they see similar rates of participation? You can also look to existing research on things like typical no-show rates for a particular service type, whether substance abuse treatment, parent training, or something else.

So, imagine for example, that you are a relatively new child and family serving agency on the west side of Chicago and have been trying somewhat unsuccessfully to deliver home-visiting services to the primarily Black, Latinx, and white clients in your service area. You may note that your overall participation rate, or the percentage of clients that accept and initiate services, is less than what you know is the average participation rate for home-visiting programs in your area—perhaps in other parts of the city or perhaps for the home-visiting field in general. So, why is this? In the next chapter, we will describe in more detail the data sources and approaches you can use to learn about the adaptation problem that will help you figure out what to do next. But perhaps your sense is that there is a general lack of trust in the community, particularly for a new agency in the area. This may be the adaptation problem you are initially trying to solve. However, let us also imagine that after doing a little more analysis, you find that generally what accounts for your low participation rate is that participation is particularly low among your Latinx clients. Perhaps there is something about the home-visiting program that is culturally incongruent with many Latinx families. Or, perhaps there is a competing service provider who is targeting the same community as your agency and have been serving the Latinx community for many years and have a stronger, more trusted reputation in the community. You could probably come up with other hypotheses as to why there is a particularly poor participation rate. Poor relative participation rates suggest that there are barriers to participation that are unique to that particular client subgroup.

Parent training interventions, for example, are quite good at engaging moms, but dads tend not to participate in high numbers. Data from parent training studies consistently indicate that fathers participate in low numbers, and for many years, the exclusion of fathers was not even recognized as a problem. Fathers were often framed as less important, absent from most families served by parent training, or even dangerous (Bellamy, 2009). However, it's a bit of a mystery as to exactly why fathers do not participate. For example, it may be that parent training is often scheduled at times or in places that are convenient for mothers, but not fathers. Or perhaps because many service providers assume

---

Box 7.1

Participation is challenging in many service contexts, so it is helpful to know whether the rate of participation you are observing is low within that context.

that fathers do not want to participate, they tend to forget to invite men. Without some data, the precise nature of the problem to be solved is unclear.

Engagement

Poor participation is not the only evidence of an adaptation problem. Alternatively, the problems may be more about poor engagement. So, clients may come to services but then fail to engage in a meaningful or constructive way. Poor engagement may be reflected by low levels of investment or active participation in the intervention, even when the client is attending. In parent training interventions, this may include limited or no contribution to group discussions, little or no effort in intervention activities, or noncompletion of homework assignments. Parents may be attending but not interacting with the clinical content in a way that is likely to result in optimal outcomes.

We will give you another example to illustrate. One of us recently interviewed some parents who were court-ordered to attend some classes as part of their efforts to be reunited with their children who were placed in foster care. All of the parents had been participating in a drug court program, but they had been assigned to different courts and different judges. They were all going because they felt they had to do so. Nearly all of parents described how they were, at first, pretty disengaged with the process. They would "go through the motions" and do what was required, but their hearts were not in it. They felt the program was not helpful, and so they were investing as little time and effort in it as possible. But, some of them were assigned to a judge who they really liked and they felt that this judge cared for them. So, they began to work harder in the program and invest themselves into the services. They were investing in the services, not just to comply because the stakes were so high, but because they felt things would get better with the help of this judge and the drug court and that someone was rooting for them. Other parents were assigned to a less engaging judge, and they never really felt like investing themselves in the service.

So, engagement is a different kind of adaptation problem. It is not about getting people in the door; it's how well you engage them in the intervention so that they can benefit from services. Evidence of an engagement might come from client satisfaction surveys or other venues through which clients might reflect on their investment, buy-in, or engagement with the service. You might also become aware of this problems through the reports of service providers who note that your clients in general or a particular subgroup of clients were not well engaged in the intervention. Just as in the case of participation, you might find that most of your clients are not well engaged in a particular intervention, or maybe just a certain subgroup is not as invested in the service. Perhaps your traditional grief counseling group is not engaging to younger clients, although it continues to get high satisfaction ratings from older clients. These suggest an engagement problem that may require some adaptations.

Efficacy

Another type of evidence that is suggestive of an adaptation problem comes from data indicating that a particular intervention is less efficacious for a particular groups of clients. Intervention outcomes may be smaller, slower in coming, poorly sustained, or even absent altogether for some clients. So, using our parent training example, even if fathers participate and engage with parent training interventions, the interventions may not target the key skills, knowledge, and attitudes that are most salient to fathers. In other words, the intervention may not meet the needs of fathers as well as they do for mothers. Given that most parent training interventions were developed with and for mothers, important dimensions related to parenting for fathers might have been excluded. There is some evidence of this in the published literature. In a meta-analysis by Lundahl, Tollefson, Risser, and Lovejoy (2007) that looked at father involvement in parent training, mothers showed greater immediate and longer-term treatment gains than fathers.

Research studies in the published literature or government reports may also be a source of evidence that, in general, an intervention works better for some clients than others. Or it may even demonstrate that the intervention generally doesn't work well for any clients overall. There are, unfortunately, several example of interventions that have been very popular and well-disseminated in practice but do not seem to help people—and may even harm them (e.g. Rhule, 2005).

Existing research indicates an adaptation problem for fathers' in terms of their participation in and benefit from parent training. It is less clear whether or not fathers' engagement in parent training represents another important dimension of the adaptation problem to be solved. Some adaptations may be more sensibly linked to one dimension or another. For example, training service providers on specific strategies to reach out to fathers may increase participation but making changes to the clinical content of an intervention so as to reflect examples or parenting activities that are more salient to fathers and fathering may improve engagement. However, it is also possible that the adaptation problem is evidenced

---

Box 7.2

Poor engagement may be reflected by low levels of investment or active participation in the intervention, even when the client is attending.

across each of these dimensions and will require adaptations to a variety of elements of the intervention.

Evidence of Adaptation Problems for Contexts

Adaptation problems may be reflective of a mismatch between the intervention context and the intervention. For example, we have worked with school social workers on occasion who have been interested in ESIs that have been developed for use in clinics and importing them into the school setting. There are, of course, some clear differences between clinic-based services and school-based services. For example, school social workers often find that they must conform their work to the limited opportunities allowed in a usual school day. So, this often means they have maybe 20 or 30 minutes to work with a child or a group of children at lunch, during homeroom, or briefly after school. Many interventions, like social skills interventions, may be designed to be delivered in longer chunks of time. So, a natural adaptation might be to split up program content that might be designed to be delivered in one session across two or more sessions.

Context-related adaptation problems often have to do with time and resources. Many of the social service agencies we have worked with in the past want to make interventions shorter to make them conform to time limits or to make them less expensive to deliver as less staff time is required. In other cases, interventions may require special tools, technology, or spaces that are not available to you. For example, Parent–Child Interaction Therapy (PCIT) was originally designed for use with a one-way mirror and a "bug in the ear," or an in-ear audio device, that was used to coach parents in real time as they interacted with their children and learned new parenting techniques. However, when home visitors started to pick up PCIT as a possible intervention to integrate into their visits, they wondered if they could use the same coaching techniques without the mirror or the bug in the ear, given that most people's homes aren't equipped with one-way mirrors and home-visiting programs may not be able to afford ear-bug technology.

In these examples, it is unlikely that there is anything much that could be done to change the context of service so that the interventions could be

---

Box 7.3

Intervention outcomes may be smaller, slower in coming, poorly sustained, or even absent altogether for some clients.

Box 7.4

Context-related adaptation problems often have to do with time and resources. Many of the social service agencies we have worked with in the
past want to make interventions shorter to make them conform to time
limits or to make them less expensive to deliver as less staff time is required.

---

delivered exactly as they were originally intended. School days are unlikely to
become freed up from time constraints, and people are unlikely to start living
in homes with one-way mirrors. So, making the adaptation to the intervention
seems a sensible approach. Or, at least worth a try. These changes are also more
"peripheral" in nature. It's true that delivering social skills group interventions
to kids in smaller chunks may diminish the intervention somehow. Maybe, for
example, there is not enough time to practice the skills that are learned. Or, perhaps PCIT is not as effective if the child can hear you coaching their parent.
But, at the end of the day, children are still being taught the same social skills
and parents are still being coached to better communication with their children. These examples also underscore the importance of evaluating intervention
outcomes before, during, and after making an adaptation. If the changes that are
made to the intervention have a significant, unacceptable impact on the efficacy
of the intervention, then it is time to look for an alternative—whether that's a
different intervention or one that is crafted specifically for the service context in
which you are working.

Again, to Adapt or Not to Adapt?

Deciding to make an adaption, whether to address the mismatch between the
intervention and the clients you service, or the context in which you serve them,
is a big decision and is helped by the insight of some research or data. The use
of qualitative data, administrative data, and analysis of existing research on the
client groups you are trying to serve can provide particularly valuable insights
as to the nature of adaptation problem, as in the previous examples. In the next
chapter, we will provide you with an overview of the different models that have
been used to guide adaptations to existing interventions and walk you through
the process. However, before we take that step, it's important to stop and consider whether or not an adaptation is really the best course of action.

There is a decent amount of research out there to suggest some caution
for three reasons. First, sometimes there is a perception of a need to adapt an

intervention, but really no evidence. Because adaptation takes an awful lot of work and there are real risks involved—particularly the risk of compromising the internal logic of an intervention—you really need to feel confident that an adaptation problem exists. Second, we have worked with some social work practitioners who look at an intervention, do not like how it looks on paper, and decide straight away they would like to change it. Our suggestion is that practitioners first get training in an intervention as it was intended, try using it for a while as it was intended, and then think about engaging in the adaptation process if needed. Sometimes interventions seem unappealing because they are unfamiliar or different from what you are accustomed to using. In other cases, the manual and training are not attractively packaged or user-friendly. These are not good reasons to adapt the intervention. You may find that over time the intervention becomes more familiar and you become more comfortable using it. You may also find that you can create supplemental trainings or manual materials to shore up the deficiencies. The other benefit of learning the intervention as it was intended is that you are going to be much more likely to recognize the core versus peripheral elements of the intervention and make wiser choices about what could be changed and what is best left alone.

Finally, one should also consider making changes that are focused not on adaptations to the intervention, but rather the other two circles in Figure 7.1. If the aim is to better align the intervention, the client, and the service context, the best strategy may be to somehow prepare or change the service context to better support the intervention, rather than change the intervention itself. You can also consider what might be done to work with client to better prepare them to benefit from the intervention. For example, you might work with a client whom you think would benefit greatly from participating in a residential substance abuse treatment program. However, perhaps they do not feel that their drug use is that big of deal. You might provide some sort of individual counseling with that client, maybe use motivational interviewing, to explore the ways in which the drug use is impacting his or her mood, relationships, and ability to maintain a job. After some work, some time, and some reflection, that same client might be interested in trying the inpatient program that was not appealing six months earlier. In this case you are not adapting the inpatient substance abuse program to serve clients who do not want to participate or do not think they need the program but rather working with your client to get them ready. You could say that that the client is adapting, not the intervention.

This is similar to the idea behind the concept of "readiness to change" based on the work of Prochaska and DiClemente (1983) and others over the last few decades. Some people simply are not in the right place along the change process to benefit from an intervention, and you may need to use other approaches such as motivational interviewing before someone can successfully participate

---

1. What is the evidence that there is an adaptation problem based on published research, administrative data from my agency, or client feedback?

2. Have you or your staff been adequately trained in the intervention you plan to adapt and have experience delivering it as intended, with a high degree of fidelity?

3. Does the service context in which you work support your ability to get training, consultation, and evaluation data that you will need to adequately support the adaptation process?

4. Have you or your staff considered alternative interventions that could be used that may not need adaptations, or may need fewer adaptations, even if they are not evidence-supported interventions?

Figure 7.2 Alternatives to adaptation.

in a substance abuse program. Similar concepts have been explored to address homelessness for example. Some approaches use a "housing first" framework, whereby clients are first provided with safe and stable housing before anything else; the idea being that before any other issues can be tackled—be it health, mental health, substance abuse, or vocational training—people first need to feel secure in their basic need for shelter.

Likely, there are several approaches that you might use to improve the fit between intervention, service context, and clients. It is worth exploring a variety of approaches and possible "next steps" before you jump into the intervention adaptation process. We suggest that you consider the alternatives outlined in Figure 7.2 before embarking on efforts to adapt an intervention.

If, after considering these questions you still feel that adapting an intervention is the best course of action, the following chapter will give you some specific approaches and models to use to identify, implement, and evaluate the adaptations that you will make to the intervention.

Discussion Questions

1. Why is it important to gather evidence on whether an adaptation problem exists before proceeding to make changes to an intervention?

2. If an intervention is not achieving the outcomes that you hope, how many different reasons can you think of that might explain the disappointing results? What type of data could you gather to find out what the problem might be?

3. What are the benefits of first learning how to do an intervention as it was intended before you proceed to make adaptations to it?

8

Intervention Adaptation Models and Example

In this chapter, we will provide an overview of some widely used adaptation models that have been proposed and suggest a common model that combines elements from each of these models. Interventions adaptation models, like much of implementation science, is relatively new. These approaches do not represent all of the adaptation models available to social work practitioners, but different adaptation models have a lot in common.

Cultural Adaptation of Interventions

As we discussed earlier in this book, one of the most well-developed areas of work on adaptation of interventions is related to adaptation for cultural subgroups. Although different people have proposed and applied slightly different frameworks and processes to the task of adapting existing interventions to better fit cultural groups, many of these frameworks and processes are similar. Barrera, Castro, Strycker, and Toobert (2013) highlight the commonalities across these frameworks and describe five stages of cultural adaptation. Figure 8.1 outlines these five stages of cultural adaption.

Information Gathering

In this stage, information is collected to inform the decision as to whether an adaptation is needed as well as what components of the intervention should be modified. The activities that are suggested as possibilities at this stage include searching the literature to see if research indicates that different cultural groups have different risk factors for outcomes that might be differentially targeted for intervention. These differences might point to a need to make adaptations to

Stage 1: Information gathering

Stage 2: Preliminary adaptation design

Stage 3: Preliminary adaptation tests

Stage 4: Adaptation refinement

Stage 5: Cultural adaptation trial

Figure 8.1 The five stages of cultural adaptation.

the mechanisms or the core elements of interventions. Berrera et al. (2013) also suggest searching the literature to see if there are differences in engagement or efficacy of the intervention for different groups. This stage also might include the collection of qualitative data from either participants or professionals who have used the intervention to gain their insight on what components of the intervention are working well and what improvements might be made for different cultural groups. By the end of this stage, a decision is made about whether cultural adaptation is necessary.

Preliminary Adaptation Design

At this stage evidence from Stage 1 is integrated to direct specific adaptations that should be made. The input of participants, practitioners, and intervention developers should be gathered in this process as well. Efforts to identify and preserve the core elements of the intervention should be made, and only those changes to core elements supported by evidence collected in Stage 1 should be made. If language adaptations are needed, then this is stage where translation and back translation of materials are also made after adjustment to core and peripheral elements are in place. Once materials are drafted in their new revised form, key stakeholders including participants, practitioners, and intervention developers should again be engaged to provide feedback on the revised components. Pilot tests of the revised intervention components may also be conducted at this stage.

Preliminary Adaptation Tests

In this stage, practitioners are trained in the full intervention, with any revised training, materials, or other supports, and these newly trained practitioners will pilot test the intervention with a limited number of clients. While the pilot testing is underway, qualitative data are collected about how the implementation is going. This is the opportunity to find out what is working well and what additional adaptations are needed. At this stage, the adaptation team may need to work with a researcher to collect and analyze data, but simple measures and metrics such as dropout rates may be used to track changes without the use any sophisticated research methods.

Adaptation Refinement

After the adapted intervention has been pilot tested and data has been collected about the process and the outcomes of the pilot, these data are reviewed to consider any additional adaptations or refinements that may need to be made. If, for example, one of the problems identified in Stage 1 was that participants in a particular subgroup were likely to drop out of the intervention, but after adaptations are made the dropout rate remains unchanged, then further adaptations are likely needed.

Cultural Adaptation Trial

Once the intervention has been refined based on pilot data, a larger traditional clinical trial can be conducted to test the intervention. This stage is really the opportunity for the evaluation of the outcomes of the adapted intervention. In addition, more sophisticated analyses can be conducted on the adapted intervention to find out if the intervention is working as planned and if it works for different subgroups such as those with different levels of acculturation. This is also another opportunity to collect more input from participants and practitioners about additional improvements or modifications. This stage really requires partnership with a researcher. This type of study is complicated and time-consuming. Because the work of Barrera et al. (2013) is reflective of the work of a researchers in partnership with practitioners and aimed to provide research evidence that could inform the field broadly, this stage is needed to collect research evidence that is *generalizable*. Although it would be wonderful for you to be able share what you learn with the field in a way that is more likely to generalize to other practitioners, organizations, and communities, you may choose to stop your work at the pilot stage once you are satisfied with the improvements you are able to achieve within your organization and with your clients.

ADAPT-ITT Model

Although adaptation of existing evidence-supported interventions (ESIs) to meet the needs of cultural groups is one area in which intervention adaptation has been well thought-through and developed, other scholars working with different populations and problems have also developed adaptation models. Another example is in the area of HIV prevention and intervention. In the late 1980s and early 1990s, the Centers for Disease Control began to identify ESIs, but also recognized that to *scale-up*, or broadly implement these interventions for wide dissemination, processes were needed to guide modifications to ESI to fit local needs and populations (Wingwood & DiClemente, 2008). The Centers for Disease Control developed a rather complicated adaptation model called the Map of the Adaptation Process, or MAP, which was subsequently adapted by Wingwood and DiClemente (2008) into an eight-phase process that could be more reasonably managed by practitioners in the community. You will notice that these phases have a lot in common with the stages previously outlined in the cultural adaptation model. This model was developed specifically for HIV interventions, and it was not aimed at addressing the needs of different cultural groups alone. Figure 8.2 outlines the eight phases of the ADAPT-ITT Model.

In the first phase of this model, information is collected through activities such as focus groups, interviews, or needs assessments to gather information about the new group's risks, intervention preferences, and their perceived need for the intervention. In the second phase, an ESI is selected, and a decision is made about whether or not the ESI should be adopted or adapted. Sound familiar? In this model, however, more attention is paid to the process of selecting the best ESI to start with based on the desired outcomes, the similarity of the population with which it has already been shown to be effective, and the capacity of the organization to mount the intervention.

Phase 1 Assessment: Who is the new target population and why is at risk of HIV?
Phase 2 Decision: What intervention is going to be selected and is it going to be adopted or adapted?
Phase 3 Administration: What in the original intervention needs to be adapted, and how should it be adapted?
Phase 4 Production: How do you produce the initial adapted intervention and document the adaptations that are made?
Phase 5 Topical Experts: Who can help adapt the intervention?
Phase 6 Integration: What is going to be included in the adapted intervention that will be piloted?
Phase 7 Training: Who needs to be trained?
Phase 8 Testing: Was the adaptation successful, and did it enhance the short-term outcomes?

Figure 8.2 The eight phases of the ADAPT-ITT model.

In the third phase of the ADAPT-ITT framework, "theater testing" is used, which is more similar to a marketing approach, where potential participants, as well as staff or other stakeholders, are presented with the potential intervention and are asked to provide their input, both individually and as a group on the ESI. These data are analyzed and used to guide the fourth phase of the process, which is to design a first draft version of the adapted ESI. This can be a highly time-consuming process, and the authors underscore the need to balance the maintenance of core elements and the internal logic of the intervention with adaptations that are made to better suit the clients and the service context at this stage. At this stage, the authors suggest making an "adaptation plan" that includes

1. The aim of the adaption plan.
2. The ESI to be adapted.
3. The publication(s) citing the ESI as effective.
4. The new target population and/or context.
5. The core elements of the original ESI.
6. The new procedures, activities, or other elements that may be more appropriate for the new target population and/or context.

In the fifth phase of ADAPT-ITT, expert consultants are brought into the process to assist with the adaptation. This could be the intervention developer or experts who have long-standing experience delivering or training on the original ESI. This could also be experts in the new population or service context. Consultants may be needed in any area central to the ESI to guide adaptations to protect the core elements and internal working logic, or you may need experts who understand or are members of the new population or context for which you are making the adaptations. It depends where your adaptations team may lack expertise.

In Stage 6, the expert consultation, data collected, and needs and capacity of the practitioners are integrated into a second draft of the adapted ESI. Then, Stages 7 and 8 involve the training and support of the practitioners who will use the adapted in intervention, and the evaluation of the adapted ESI's implementation, including a smaller pilot followed by a larger more rigorous test of the intervention. This is similar to the last two phases of Berrara et al.'s (2013) model. You or your team may be able to conduct a pilot with or without consultation, but a larger study would require partnership or engagement with researchers. It depends again on whether you want to apply your findings to your practice only or want to develop research evidence that is more generalizable.

General Adaptation Processes and Example

As we discussed earlier, there are several different examples of adaptations models and frameworks that could be used to guide the adaptation of a specific ESI. In this example, we will illustrate the use of adaptation of a parent training intervention created primarily for mothers to better serve fathers. Although this example does not employ either the cultural adaptation model or the previously described ADAPT-ITT model, it employs steps and processes common to both and also includes some additional approaches that we think will be helpful in clarifying what exactly the adaptation problem is in your case. We integrate the common factors framework here to help you think through the pieces of the intervention that may require adaptation to address the adaptation problem.

The four steps in our suggested general process are (a) specification of the adaptation problem in terms of participation, engagement, and/or efficacy; (b) identification of adaptation targets across model and technique, relationship, expectancy, and extratherapeutic factors; (c) application of the adaptations to the intervention; and (d) testing of adaptations for improvements across recruitment and retention, engagement, or efficacy outcomes.

Step 1: Specification of the Adaptation Problem

Throughout this book, we have used examples from our own work including research and practice approaches designed to better serve fathers in child and family interventions. You may have a hunch that evidence-supported parenting interventions do not work well for dads, but you likely do not have a firm handle on the research literature on father engagement in parent training. This research may provide some insight as to whether there is indeed an adaptation problem to be solved and what that problem may be exactly. Parent training interventions are built from a lot of different elements, and without some guidance as to what you should adapt, you are just making guesses and likely to wasting precious time and resources.

Is There a Need to Adapt?

Our first step here is to take a look at the existing research on parent training for fathers to see if we have an adaptation problem, either as evidenced by problems in participation, engagement, efficacy, or fit with the service context as described in Chapter 7 (this volume). In this case, data from parent training studies consistently indicates that fathers participate in parent training in low numbers.

For example, a systematic review of literature examining father engagement in behavioral parent training for attention-deficit/hyperactivity disorder showed extremely low rates of participation, and 87% of the studies identified do not include any information on father-related outcomes (Fabiano, 2007). Other studies have similarly highlighted similarly low rates of father participation in parenting interventions (Bagner & Eyberg, 2003; Panter-Brick et al., 2014; Tiano & McNeil, 2005). Existing research has less information to contribute in terms of insights into problems related to engagement when fathers do participate. It may be possible that we may need to address multiple adaptation problems. In one of the few empirical studies examining the adaptation of parent training for fathers, Fabiano et al. (2012) found that their adaptation to parent training using a team-sport approach to deliver the core elements of parent training resulted in the development and maintenance of father engagement. In terms of adaptation problems related to efficacy, a meta-analysis that looked at father involvement in parent training, mothers showed greater immediate and longer-term treatment gains than fathers (Lundahl, Tollefson, Risser, & Lovejoy, 2007). Tucker, Gross, Fogg, Delaney, and Lapporte (1998) specifically showed that outcomes were smaller and mostly absent for fathers and none of the outcomes were maintained at one year after the intervention ended.

Based on our observations as practitioners and the research evidence in the area, there does appear to be a need to adapt parent training to better serve fathers. And likely there is a participation and efficacy problem to be solved and possibly an engagement problem as well. You may find yourself working in an area where there is little or no research evidence in place to inform the challenges related to participation, engagement, and efficacy; rather, you'll need to collect your own data, maybe from administrative records or perhaps through a needs assessment or the collection and analysis of other data such as interviews or focus groups with clients.

Have Adaptations Been Tested?

Although many intervention adaptation models recommend gathering data, not many mention searching the literature to identify existing recommendations for adaptations to an interventions. There may even be research that has tested pieces of the adaptation that you are thinking about making. In the case of adaptations to parent training to better serve fathers, there were a great deal of different ideas described in the literature about how to better engage and serve fathers through parent training, but very little empirical evidence to support any of them. These ideas were just opinions. So, based on the existing research literature, we had a whole lot of ideas about what adaptations could be made but no research to help decide which adaptations were the best bet.

> ### Box 8.1
>
> Even if existing research pointed to some promising possibilities, it is critical to get feedback from stakeholders. This includes the people who are expert in the unadapted intervention, those who will be trained to use the intervention, and those who will participate in the intervention.

Step 2: Identification of Adaptation Targets Across Technique, Relationship, Expectancy, and Extratherapeutic Factors

At this stage in the process additional data and expert guidance are needed to guide the adaptation process. Because the existing research produced ideas about adaptation but no clear guidance on which adaptations to parent training would be most promising to implement, we decided to collect qualitative data from experts who might have some insight. Even if existing research pointed to some promising possibilities, it is critical to get feedback from stakeholders. This includes the people who are expert in the unadapted intervention, those who will be trained to use the intervention, and those who will participate in the intervention.

To do so, our research team interviewed 20 parent training intervention developers, researchers, and clinicians. We asked these experts to describe their experience working with fathers in parent training and to suggest changes to parent training intervention that would potentially increase fathers' participation in, engagement with, and benefit from parent training. In addition, we conducted two focus groups with fathers and asked for their expert insights on what they would like to get from parent training intervention. Then we organized their feedback by techniques (core and peripheral elements), expectancy, extratherapeutic, and relationship factors to illustrate the possible adaptations under each factor as they were described by the experts.

Techniques

Core Elements

As we discussed earlier in this book, there is a real concern that adaptations do not change the internal logic of an intervention or at least not do so without good reason. Overall, the experts that we interviewed felt that the core elements of the existing evidence-supported parent training models were generally applicable to both mothers and fathers and no adaptation was needed to change the core elements of interventions.

The components of parent training interventions that were most important to the experts, also reflected those elements described by Kaminski, Valle, Filene, and Boyle (2008) as the standard parent training content. A few experts did suggest changes to the core elements of parent training interventions, but they all suggested adding, rather than removing, elements that are not currently represented in evidence-supported parent training models. The three most comment content areas that experts suggested adding for fathers were (a) techniques designed to encourage fathers' reflection on parenting and being parented, (b) techniques designed to increase fathers' emotional awareness and how to manage feelings, and (c) techniques designed to improve the mother–father or co-parenting relationships.

Peripheral Elements

Most of the changes to the clinical content of parent training that were recommended by the parent training experts related to the peripheral elements of parent training interventions. These adaptations included using father-inclusive or gender-neutral images and language throughout the intervention including videos, worksheets, and other materials related to recruitment for or delivery of the intervention. Others described the importance of labeling the parent training as something other than "training" or a "class" since some fathers have a negative reaction to these terms. Interviewees felt these words suggested that there was something wrong with fathers' parenting, whereas other felt fathers had bad experiences with schools or learning in traditional environments. Less problematic words included "program" or "group." One interviewee recommended simplifying the programs as much as possible, and another mentioned the need to make sure that the reading level was not too high, especially for low-income fathers.

Some interviewees made suggestions about adaptations to the order in which clinical content is presented to parents. These changes to the order included delivering the topics that are most appealing to fathers first. Another possible adaptation was to provide options to fathers as to where or how to start parent training. For example, fathers may be offered a brief seminar providing an overview of parent training first and then enter a traditional parent training group. Another interviewee suggested running a fathers-only parent training group first, followed by a couples-based parent training group as a follow-up. These approaches are intended to provide an opportunity to deliver male-focused parent training content such as those previously described topics or give fathers a chance to get exposure to and practice engaging in a group-based parenting intervention without the added pressure or intimidation involved in participating with mothers in a traditional group.

Parent training experts also discussed changing the *dosage* or amount of parent training interventions; nearly all suggested shortening the intervention to better serve fathers. Interviewees recommended bringing the interventions down to 10 weeks, 6 weeks, or even just one session. The idea of thinking about dosing from a family perspective was also described. For example, one interviewee felt that it won't always be possible to get both parents to come to all sessions. One possible approach would be to select key sessions or core elements that fathers should get if at all possible and make concentrated efforts to get fathers and mothers to both come to those.

Expectancy

The fathers and parent training adaptation problem can also be framed as an expectancy problem. Many different expectations, attitudes, and experiences might impact fathers' expectations about parent training and impact their willingness buy-in to such an intervention. For example, fathers may have few experiences with parenting interventions or negative experiences with social services, interventions, and helping professionals. They might hold traditional gender norm-based views about men's and women's roles in the home and therefore see interventions aimed at parenting to be for mothers, not fathers. Some may not feel that parent training will work or be worth the time and effort it will take to participate.

Adapting parent training using motivation and preparation strategies that target fathers' buy in or expectancy to support recruitment and engagement of fathers in parent training were described by many interviewees. Oftentimes interviewees talked about these strategies as happening on the front end of services, prior to in the beginning of the initiation of parent training. Experts described the need to clearly and firmly ask fathers to participate and then to express a lot of excitement and encouragement when they do attend.

The delivery of these motivational messages to fathers and mothers prior to, and throughout the parent training, was another adaptation commonly described by interviewees. These messages often included the same basic themes around either the unique benefits of fathers' involvement with their children or the importance of fathers' participation in parent training. Fathers should also be provided with the message that they aren't doing anything wrong, but that parent training will give them some new specialized skills to build on what they are already doing.

Extratherapeutic

Another factor to consider are those influences outside of the father, intervention, provider, or organization that might present barriers to the father's ability to participate in and engage with parent training. Fathers, like mothers, have a lot of other competing demands on their time and have complex lives. These other things might include employment, childcare responsibilities (possibly in more than one family), and relationships with friends and family members. These extratherapeutic factors place demands on fathers' time and can interact with the delivery of parent training services in other important ways. For example, mothers may or may not be supportive of his engagement in parent training. He may also be facing other challenges such as lack of education, unemployment, substance use problems, or mental health issues that prevent him from fully or successfully engaging in parent training interventions.

Addressing, acknowledging, or overcoming contextual barriers to participation often presented by extratherapeutic factors were the most commonly described approaches to increasing fathers' participation in services. One interviewee described this as "barrier busting." This included providing transportation to the sessions, making arrangements for childcare (which, on expert noted, is often overlooked for fathers), and scheduling sessions in the evenings or weekends so that working fathers can attend.

Interviewees often described helping fathers overcome extratherapeutic barriers by providing incentives. This approach does not address the barriers directly but can make parent training feel more immediately and concretely rewarding and worth the effort needed to attend parent training in the face of many other competing demands or factors that might impede his participation and engagement. Likewise, mothers may be incentivized to support fathers' participation. Incentives might include payments or points that could be used toward the purchase of items that fathers would find attractive, such as toys or supplies for their children or discounts on childcare or other services. Small tokens like graduation certificates and T-shirts were also described. One expert described a program that required fathers to participate in a parent training group before they could play basketball in a desirable league for men in the community. The provision of food was also highlighted by a number of experts, not just as an incentive, but also as a method for creating community or a comfortable and nurturing atmosphere, thus also contributing to the relational success of the intervention.

Relationship

Finally, some of the interviewees describe adaptations that would fall under the relationship factor. Parenting programs are often staffed by women, and research in a variety of areas suggests that women are unsure of, or in some cases actively avoid, working with men. This tendency may be amplified for low-income adolescent fathers who are often painted in a negative light. Although the relationship factor is described by Asay and Lambert (2008) as the interaction between the service provider and the client, we believe that this concept can be expanded to the organizational level whereby the leadership, staff, and physical characteristics of the organization also set the stage for fathers' engagement in and benefit from services.

Interviewees described the need to implement father friendliness training, not just for workers who provided services directly to fathers, but the entire staff. Interviewees also suggested hiring more male workers or clinicians, or even fathers themselves, to recruit participants, mentor other fathers, or help facilitate the parent training. Experts expressed different opinions about the gender of parent training group facilitators or leaders. Some felt men were best suited to lead parent training for fathers, others advocated for male–female teams, and still others felt either men or women could facilitate successfully.

In terms of what level adaptation should occur at, some said that the adaptation isn't really important at the mother–father level, but more so at the individual parent level. The key, they said, was to personalize and individualize your approach for each parent and to connect with each father one on one. In other words, use a *clinical tailoring* as we described in Chapter 6 (this volume) to account for individual fathers' preferences and characteristics. Similarly, others suggested that the key was the ability to build a relationship with the father, or a therapeutic alliance, as well as a safe and supportive group atmosphere.

At this stage we also conducted a focus group with mothers and fathers who were currently receiving services at a child and family serving agency with whom we were partnering. We asked these about their ideas on how they felt about including fathers in parent training services and what strategies they would use to increase fathers' participation.

Step 3: Application of the Adaptations to the Intervention

At this stage we worked with a smaller group of practitioners at our partner agency who wished to increase the participation and engagement of fathers in their evidence-supported parent training intervention. We formed a "creative team" including those who were trained in and had delivered standard parent training to review the research evidence and the data collected from experts on possible adaptations. We met over several weeks to discuss possible adaptations that could be feasibly implemented, recognizing that not all of the previously described possible adaptations could likely be addressed.

We ultimately settled on the formulation of four adaptations. These adaptations together addressed all four factors. First, we decided to add one core element, co-parenting techniques designed to improve the mother–father relationship. This was in part based on the expert interviews but also on recent research that indicated that this co-parenting relationship would likely improve intervention outcomes. In addition, we conducted some focus groups with mothers and fathers who clearly stated they wanted to participate in the intervention together, not separately as some experts had suggested. Also, infused in throughout the intervention, including within the new co-parenting core element and throughout the standard intervention content, we inserted new motivating messages designed to improve the expectancy factor of both mothers and fathers. These motivating messages were designed to increase mothers' and fathers' buy-in to the idea that their families would reap the greatest benefit from the intervention if they both attended the sessions and worked together as a team. We chose this approach because it could be easily applied to the intervention and would not take a great deal of extra time or training. In addition, our team aimed to reduce barriers presented by extratherapeutic factors by providing transportation and childcare and reducing any other barriers that might get in the way of either or both parents' participation. The father experts interviewed strongly underscored these practical barriers, and parents in our focus group also pointed to these issues, so we decided this was an important adaptation that could have significant payoffs if it cleared the way for fathers and mothers to participate together. Without addressing these barriers, we worried that we would not have a chance to deliver the intervention to both parents. And finally, we organized an additional training for staff to increase their awareness of our findings, goals to include fathers more successfully in parent training, and skill them up in the adapted intervention. This adaptation was designed to target the relationship factor.

Step 4: Testing of Adaptations for Improvements Across Recruitment and Retention, Engagement, and/or Efficacy Outcomes

To pilot test the adaptation we collected data first from one group of parents who were participating in the agency's standard parent training intervention. Then, we implemented the adapted parent training intervention, and we collected data from the parents who participated in the new version of the intervention as well. We looked at rates of participation for both mothers and fathers, measured their engagement by asking fathers and mothers to fill out a short survey at the end of each parent training session, and assessed intervention outcomes including parenting stress, the quality of their parenting, and the mother–father relationship both before and after the intervention by having each parent complete a survey. We also assessed the general feasibility of the intervention by interviewing the practitioners who implemented the intervention to gain their insight.

In terms of participation, we found that fathers did not participate in any of the sessions using the standard parent training intervention. But, in the adapted intervention, fathers participated in about 50% of the sessions. Not only that, but mothers' participation was also increased from 50% to 75%! Woo hoo! We also found that fathers, mothers, and practitioners rated the sessions as highly engaging. The outcomes, however, were more mixed. While both mothers and fathers showed reduced parenting stress in the adapted intervention as compared to the standard intervention, the adapted intervention didn't result in better parenting or better mother–father relationships as compared to the standard intervention.

So, where to go from here? Well, now at this stage it was time to take stock and reassess. Ultimately, we would like to see the adapted intervention not only increase participation and engagement but also outcomes for parents. So, the next step is to further revise the adapted intervention based on these data and consider additional adaptations that may be made. Once those improvements are determined, we can again implement and assess whether we are solving the adaptation problems that we had identified. This is an iterative process and may take several more rounds of refinement and testing before we feel we've settled on the best adaptation possible.

We hope this example provides you with a practical, feasible approach to determining whether you are facing an adaptation problem and the basic steps that need to be completed to identify the problem and produce potential solutions to address the problem or problems identified. We want to re-emphasize here that adaptation is not to be entered into lightly and that data, collaboration, and evaluation are all critical elements of the process.

Discussion Questions

1. What are the key elements of data or information that are needed to inform what adaptations should be made to an existing ESI and where can you get this data or information?
2. What strategies can be used to protect the core elements of an intervention during the adaptation process?
3. Why should a small pilot be used to first test an adapted intervention before evaluating outcomes in a larger study?

9

Fidelity

Once you have settled on the intervention that you want to use in practice, whether you have selected one "off the shelf," adapted one to better suit your needs, or built one from the ground up, the successful implementation of high-quality interventions requires specific strategies to make sure that the intervention is being done correctly and consistently well over time. We have mentioned this before, but it bears mentioning again that monitoring fidelity is helpful for a variety of reasons, including verification of adequate training, maintenance of high-quality services, and identification of problems related to implementation versus the content of the intervention itself.

First, strategies that support fidelity give you a way to measure whether anyone newly trained in an intervention has been sufficiently trained to deliver the intervention as intended. So, each time you bring on board a new staff member or learn a new intervention yourself, the fidelity checking process gives you a way to verify whether you or your colleagues are ready to use the intervention in practice with clients. Not everyone learns a new intervention at the same pace. By checking fidelity and identifying where fidelity is not strong, additional training, supervision, or other supports can be provided. Second, monitoring fidelity gives you a tool with which to ensure that a high level of quality is maintained over time. There is a very common tendency for interventions to drift away from their intended processes and procedures. A mentor of ours once said, "What is measured is what matters." It is just not enough to trust that once someone is properly trained in an intervention they will simply continue to deliver it as you would hope or expect. Most social work practitioners have competing demands on their time and attention; they often learn a variety of new programs and procedures over time. Without a consistent feedback loop whereby attention in continuously refocused on the correct application of the intervention, little by little, practices are likely to drift. Finally, continuously monitoring fidelity provides insight as to whether any disappointing client outcomes are related to a failure of the intervention to meet the needs of a client or community or a failure on the part of the provider to implement and maintain the intervention with a

---

Box 9.1

What is measured is what matters.

---

high degree of quality. Without some certainty that the intervention is being done well, it doesn't make sense to provide the client with a different intervention when the problem may be that the client received a crummy or incomplete version of the intervention.

Defining Fidelity

In this book, we have referred to fidelity quite a bit. Recall that fidelity to an intervention relates to the degree to which an intervention, in practice, reflects the standards in content, quality, and frequency of the needed to achieve optimal outcomes. Or more simply, fidelity is the degree to which interventions are provided as they were intended to be provided. Fidelity is not just important for ESI. Regardless of whether an intervention you wish to implement is or is not evidence-supported, you want people to use it correctly. So, attending to fidelity is of concern to anyone who wishes to support the implementation of an intervention to a particular set of standards.

Fidelity for All Interventions

For example, imagine that you create a new intervention designed to improve elders' comfort with computers and social network technology as a strategy to increase their social support and reduce the risk for loneliness and depression. As you develop your intervention, you may find that it is very important that older adults first get three sessions of training in basic computer skills. If, instead you jump ahead to show them social network websites and applications, they may become quickly overwhelmed and disengage from the intervention. Some important elements of fidelity measurement, in this example, might be to check whether the computer skills component was delivered before the components that introduce elders to social network websites and applications. Your colleague at another agency may catch wind of your work and get pretty excited to try out your intervention with their clients as well. So you kindly share your materials with them and explain how the intervention works. But, lo and behold, your colleague comes back to you after a few months of using the intervention and is disappointed with the results. Your colleague claims that your intervention does not work at all for their clients, who in fact just stop coming after just one or two sessions. After further discussion you learn that your colleague felt they just could not spend three sessions on basic computer skills, so they condensed the basic computer skills component to just one session. So, do you think that your intervention did not work for his clients? Or, was it that your colleague did not uphold fidelity to your intervention, and that's the real problem?

Strategies Used to Monitor Fidelity

Although it is easy to understand fidelity matters and has important implications for achieving intervention goals, there is certain a lack of uniformity as to how fidelity is measured and understood (Gearing, El-Bassel, Ghesquirer, Baldwin, Gillies, & Ngeow, 2011). Here we will provide some examples of different approaches to measuring fidelity in the field, including some of their strengths and limitations. Depending on considerations such as resources, complexity, and flexibility of the intervention and the stakes involved, a number of these approaches may be included in any particular fidelity effort. For example, it may not be realistic for a small social service agency or a single practitioner to use some of the more sophisticated and time-consuming approaches in practice. Also, some interventions are more complex than others and require more robust monitoring and feedback loops to users to ensure that practitioners have the skill and support to implement the intervention correctly. And some interventions are more tolerant of deviations from standardized practices and will produce good outcomes even with a little bit of drift.

In addition, when the stakes are high—for example, the outcomes targeted by the intervention have clear and significant impacts on clients—a more robust approach to fidelity may be needed. Many social service organizations run multiple interventions, and it may not be feasible to use a multicomponent fidelity approach for every single one. For example, it may be more important to focus fidelity efforts on interventions that aim to reduce the risk for suicide, keep children out of foster care, or intervene with interpersonal violence than interventions designed to help folks manage their time well.

Self-Report Instruments

Some strategies to monitor fidelity are pretty straight forward. Many approaches to measurement of fidelity include some sort of self-report measure. These different types of tools measures of knowledge, checklists, Likert scales, or case

> Example Question 1: 'It is best not to try to reason with people having delusions.'
> (True)
>
> Example Question 2: 'If someone has a traumatic experience, it is best to make them talk about it as soon as possible. (False)

Figure 9.1 Examples of questions designed to measure intervention knowledge.

formulations. We will talk about each one of these approaches, provide some examples, and explore their benefits and limitations.

Knowledge of an Intervention

In some cases fidelity instruments might seek to measure a practitioner's knowledge a particular intervention. This approach might be most useful in examining whether a practitioner has gained core values, tenets, or knowledge of basic practices of an intervention following training. While knowledge may indicate whether someone is generally familiar with an intervention, this knowledge does not automatically translate into actual practice behaviors. So this approach alone does not provide very deep insight into what a practitioner is actually doing in practice. Testing practitioners' knowledge of an intervention may be as simple as a number of true or false questions. In the example in Figure 9.1, the following questions were taken from a measure designed to examine the knowledge of participants in a mental health first aid training program (Caza, 2010). The participants were asked to report whether each of 20 similar questions was true or false.

Questions may be written in a simply true or false format, or they can be designed as multiple choice, fill in the blank, short answer questions, or some combination of all of these in an effort to gauge the degree to which the practitioner has accurate knowledge about an intervention.

Competency

Self-report instruments may also ask practitioners to report how competent they feel in using a particular intervention. For example, Mills and Yoshihama (2002) measured practitioners' perceived competency in working with battered women after a training. Participants were asked to report how competent they felt in carrying out the skills and practices targeted in the training including identifying battered women, effectively intervening in cases of domestic violence, and advocating on behalf of battered women. Although feelings of competence are related to whether someone can perform an intervention, much like measures of knowledge, this approach does not directly measure how well practitioners are implementing the intervention in practice. This approach may be more useful in gauging the success of the intervention in training practitioners to ready them to deliver an intervention.

Case Examples

Self-report tools may also employ a case example, or case formula, that would require the practitioners to read a case example and write about how they would apply the intervention with that particular client. This is a bit more sophisticated approach to assessing practitioners' knowledge of an intervention, insofar as they must apply their understanding of the intervention to a hypothetical case. However, this still captures what they would do, or think they should do, rather than what they are actually doing in practice. So, yes, we might gain some insight as to the degree that the practitioner's training has conveyed an understanding of what the intervention entails, but we don't really know what they might pull off in practice. For example, we can tell you very clearly what the components of motivational interviewing (MI) include, because we have read a lot about it. We have also looked at training manuals and other materials, and we've attended a basic training in the intervention. So, we could probably wing it pretty convincingly on a case example—particularly if we were given some time to sit, think, and reflect on it. And, you could grade us on how right or wrong we were in what we think we should do with a client. But could we do MI in practice? Probably not. We have never tried! We have never practiced using MI, and we have never received critical feedback on our use of MI. Given some time we could probably write you a nice technical paper about how to fly to the moon too—but we would not count on that happening with any great success either.

Checklists

A more direct approach to understanding what is actually being done in practice is to ask intervention users to report on their behavior, rather than their knowledge. A common approach to reporting practice behaviors is through a checklist. These checklists prompt the intervention user to report on whether and, if so, the degree to which the user is employing specific components of the intervention. One example of such a checklist is provided in Figure 9.2. This fidelity checklist was developed for the Dads Matter-HV intervention we described early in the book. This checklist is called the Parent Service Log (PSL), an intervention designed to engage fathers in standard home-visiting services. Since fathers have historically been poorly engaged in evidence-based

PARENT SERVICE
LOG

DATE OF CONTACT: __/ __/ __ 20   TYPE OF CONTACT: ☐Phone ☐Face-to-face
__/ ___   ☐Other (specify:

Month   Day   Year   _____)

WHO DID YOU WORK WITH DURING THIS CONTACT? (Check ✓ all that apply)
☐ Biological mother (of at least one child)   ☐ Target child/children
☐ Biological father (of at least one child)   ☐ Other
(specify:_____)

Father	Mother	ASSESSMENT
		Assessed risks and strengths associated with the mother-fother relationship
		Assessed father's risks and strengths
		Assessed whether or not father and mother are able to participate in visits together

		FATHER ENGAGEMENT
		Provided something specifically to the father (information, materials, activity, note) during or after the visit
		Personally invited the father to attend the next visit in person or through a phone call, email or letter to him
		Addressed barriers (scheduling, transportation, etc.) that make it difficult for the father to participate
		Told the parent how helpful it is to have both mothers and fathers participate in services when possible

		ROLES AND EXPECTATIONS
		Helped the parent identify his or her own parenting roles and expectations
		Discussed the parent's understanding of the other parent's roles and expectations
		Provided parent with information about how fathers' positive parenting helps child development

		COMMUNICATION
		Discussed communication styles and challenges in the mother-father parenting relationship
		Provided the parent with tips about good communication skills
		Practiced communication skills with the parent using an activity or role play

		GOAL SETTING
		Helped the parent identify his or her goals for the child
		Pointed out to the parent how the other parent's goals for the child are similar to their own

		Discussed with the parent **how their own parenting can help reach the goals** they have for their child
		Helped the parent **identify his or her own parenting goals**
		PROBLEM-SOLVING
		Discussed the parent's own **problem-solving strategies and challenges** related to parenting
		Provided the parent with **tips on good problem solving skills**
		Practiced parenting problem-solving with the parent using an activity or role play
		STRESS MANAGEMENT
		Discussed sources of parenting stress with the parent
		Provided the parent with information on the symptoms, impact, and management of stress
		Helped the parent practice stress management techniques using an activity or role play
		HELP SEEKING
		Discussed help seeking needs and challenges with the parent
		Provided the parent with information or tips on formal and informal help-seeking strategies
		Helped the parent practice help-seeking skills or strategies using an activity or role play
		ANGER MANAGEMENT
		Discussed parent's experience with anger, it's impact on parenting, and anger management strategies
		Provided the parent with information on the impact of anger on parenting and anger management tips and strategies
		Helped the parent practice anger management skills using an activity or role play
		Helped the parent identify his or her own parenting goals
		PROBLEM-SOLVING
		Discussed the parent's own problem-solving strategies and challenges related to parenting
		Provided the parent with tips on good problem solving skills

Mark with a check ✓ any of the following you did during your contact with the child's *biological mother and/or father*

Figure 9.2 Parent service log. *Source*: N. B. Guterman, J. L. Bellamy, & A. Banman, 2016, *Parent services log*. Chicago, IL: Author.

home-visiting services, Dads Matter-HV is designed to be integrated into standard service to increase father-inclusive assessment and engagement practices, as well as co-parenting content to help parenting partners work more successfully together.

In this case, the fidelity instrument relies completely on the report of the home visitors who may be implementing Dads Matter-HV in practice. A checklist-style fidelity instrument like this might include information about the date and duration of the interaction with the client as well as which clients were present for the intervention. In the case of Dads Matter-HV, the intervention is built to so that some content is delivered in a particular order, with assessment and father engagement activities preceding other components. So it would be important to look at the date of the interaction, as well as PSLs, which record the clinical content to verify that the components are being delivered to the clients in the correct order. Since Dads Matter-HV directs home visitors who to use the assessment process in their earliest visits, if we see that a home visitor is not using assessment until the fourth or fifth visit, then they are not using the intervention with fidelity. The PSL also includes information about who was present during the intervention because Dads Matter-HV is a family intervention for mother–father couples wherein both parents are targeted for inclusion. So both the mom and the dad should be included in the assessment to maintain fidelity to the intervention. The majority of the checklist provides an opportunity for users to indicate which clinical components they used with the parents in any given interaction. There are certainly limitations to this approach to monitoring fidelity. For example, we can tell if home visitors report the use of assessments with mom and dad, as well as roughly when they used these components, but we can't see anything about the quality of this particular part of the intervention. Type of contact is also recorded, because although Dads Matter-HV can be delivered by phone, face-to-face contacts are preferred over other modalities.

While the PSL captures many important elements of the intervention that we and our colleagues believe to be important, including the order of the intervention elements, which parents are included in the intervention, and which elements are provided, you will notice that this tool really doesn't assess the quality with which these intervention elements are delivered. So yes, we went to the moon—but how long did it take to get there? Did everyone survive? Did everyone get back to Earth? Checklist-style fidelity tools like this give some information about what was given to whom and when, but we won't know how well the user actually was able to do things like assess risks and strengths or how adequately they addressed barriers, for example. If you want to be able to capture quality, other strategies to fidelity measurement are likely needed.

Likert Scales

Fidelity instruments have been designed to elicit information about how practitioners are using an intervention in a variety of different ways. Checklists, such as the previous example, are common. But, in other cases, a Likert scale may be used. *Likert scales* measure agreement or degree by asking reporters to select a number or a word that best represents their experience or perception. Likert scales can elicit more nuanced information about the frequency, quality, or the nature of intervention procedures. So, they assess not just whether the practitioner used assessment, engagement, or problem-solving techniques, but also how often they were used or with what level of quality they were used.

One of the items on the PSL asks the practitioner to report whether the worker, "addressed barriers (scheduling, transportation, etc.) that make it difficult for the father to participate." This item might be transformed into a Likert scale item that assess the frequency with which the risks and strengths were assessed or one that assessed the quality with which the assessment was performed. Figure 9.3 provides examples how this item might be rewritten in a Likert scale format to capture these elements of the intervention component, rather than just whether the intervention component was used at all. Ideally workers would continuously

---

How often did you address barriers (scheduling, transportation, etc.) that make it difficult for the father to participate?

1. Every visit with the family

2. Most visits with the family

3. Some visits with the family

4. One or two visits with the family

5. No visits with the family

To what degree did you use the instructions and the materials provided in the manual to address barriers (scheduling, transportation, etc.) that make it difficult for the father to participate?

1. I did not talk to the mother or father about barriers.

2. I talked to the father or mother about barriers, but I did not use any of the tools in the manual to reduce barriers.

3. I talked to the father or mother about barriers, and I used tools in the manual for reducing barriers.

4. I talked to both the mother and father about barriers, and I used tools in the manual for reducing barriers.

Figure 9.3 Examples of Likert scales items that assess frequency and quality.

address barriers to fathers' participation and ask what could be done to make it easier for him to attend home visits. So, the more frequently a worker indicated that barriers were being addressed in the home visits, the greater the fidelity is to the model. In the second example item, workers are also asked to indicate whether they are addressing barriers with both mothers and fathers and whether they are using tools in provided in the manual to do so. The higher the score, the greater the fidelity is.

These different types of tools, including checklists, Likert scales, measures of knowledge, or case examples, may be monitored by supervisors, or in the case where practitioners are seeking certification in a particular intervention, these checklists may be submitted to a trainer, consultant, or intervention developer who will assess where there is an acceptable level of fidelity to the model achieved or being maintained. These folks can also use these checklists to guide the feedback or the supervision that they provide to practitioners who are using the intervention.

Observation

At the end of the day, all of these self-measures are limited in the information that they can provide regarding fidelity. They all rely on the practitioner being able to accurately assess their own knowledge and behaviors, and, unfortunately, current evidence seems to suggest that practitioners in a variety of allied professions have a limited ability to self-assess their competence in practice (e.g., Davis et al., 2006; Love, Koob, & Hill, 2007). In some cases, supervisors, trainers, or consultants may use observation to determine whether a practitioner is using an intervention as designed. This is the gold standard approach to assessing fidelity. There are several different strategies through which observers might collect data to rate practitioners on their fidelity to an intervention. The practitioner may be asked to audio record or video record their use of an intervention over a specific amount of time with a specific number of clients, groups, or client interactions. For example, if you were seeking certification in the Incredible Years model of parent training, a group-based parenting intervention, you would have to audio record your delivery of Incredible Years with at least two groups. There may be other requirements as well, such as the minimum number of clients who must complete the group sessions. In other cases, practitioners' use of an intervention may be directly observed through a one-way mirror or through the use of a co-facilitator, or even client reports of their experience in receiving the intervention.

Figure 9.4 provides another example of a section of a fidelity assessment tool that is meant to be used by an observer. This just one section of a longer tool designed to rate practitioners' competencies in using MI. Notice that this

MOTIVATIONAL INTERVIEWING
ADHERENCE AND COMPETENCE FEEDBACK FORM

	MI Consistent Items	Adherence Rating*								Competence Rating**							
		1	2	3	4	5	6	7		NA	1	2	3	4	5	6	7
1	MI Style or Spirit																
2	Open-ended Questions																
3	Affirmations of Strengths & Self-efficacy																
4	Reflective Statements																
5	Fostering Collaboration																
6	Motivation to Change																
7	Developing Discrepancies																
8	Pros, Cons and Ambivalence																
9	Change Planning Discussion																
10	Client-Centered Problem Discussion and Feedback																
	MI Inconsistent Items																
11	Unsolicited Advice, Directions & Feedback																
12	Emphasize Abstinence																
13	Direct Confrontation																
14	Powerlessness, Loss of Control																
15	Asserting Authority																
16	Closed-Ended Questions																

*ADHERENCE: 1 — Not at all 2 — A little 3 — infrequent 4 — Somewhat 5 — 'Quite a bit 6- Considerably 7 — Extensively" COMPETENCE: 1 — Very poor 2- Poor 3 — Acceptable 4 — Adequate 5 — Good 6 Very Good 7 - Excellent

Figure 9.4 Motivational interviewing fidelity tool example section. *Source:* S. Martino, S. A. Ball, S. L. Gallon, D. Hall, S. Ceperich, C. Farentinos, …W. Hausotter, 2006, *Motivational interviewing assessment: Supervisory tools for enhancing proficiency.* Salem, OR: Northwest Frontier Addiction Technology Transfer Center, Oregon Health and Science University.

tool elicits information from the rater about style and spirit, as well as the competency in the use of specific strategies. This tool also seeks to capture both practices that are consistent with MI and those that are not consistent with MI. This way the observer can guide the user in improving or strengthening the use of practices that are aligned with MI and also work to eliminate those practice that are counter to MI. Although it is possible for a practitioner to self-rate their competency on a tool such as this, we know that they are likely to be biased. For example, a practitioner may be tempted to rate themselves as more competent than they really are or, alternatively, may be overly critical. In addition, if the practitioner is not yet competent in MI, it is much more difficult for them to recognized practices that are or are not consistent with MI. These tools require expertise in the intervention itself, as well as training in how to properly use the fidelity tool.

If audio or video recordings are being used to check for fidelity, the practitioner then provides the recordings to the observer. Whether recordings are used, direct observations through a one-way mirror or some similar strategy are used, the trainer, supervisor, or consultant often uses a tool, such as the one provided in Figure 9.4, to determine the degree to which the practitioner is implementing the intervention with fidelity. The practitioner will then be provided with feedback based on these observations and ratings. Whether the fidelity checking process is being completed through self-report, or by observations, the practitioner may be asked to repeat the process until their use of the intervention meets a certain level of competency and may be asked to periodically engage in fidelity checking to protect against drift and get some support or training in areas that may need to be improved.

Benefits and Challenges of Self-Report and Observational Fidelity Strategies

The formality of the process, the stringency of the requirements, and the cost of receiving ratings and feedback varies across intervention models. Generally speaking, however, using observation to monitor fidelity is more expensive and time-consuming than self-report strategies. The preferred approach to monitoring fidelity is determined by the intervention developer, who have different philosophies about how closely they wish to monitor and maintain fidelity. In some cases, intervention developers seek to maintain tight control over who is certified to use their intervention, and users who wish to become certified may even receive feedback and evaluations from the very person who created the intervention. In other cases, particularly with interventions that are more widely disseminated, there are other trainers and consultants who have been certified to teach and evaluate the quality of the implementation of an intervention.

The focus of the self-report or observational measures of fidelity can also vary, but observation is more likely to give you more nuanced and less biased information about the quality of the interaction between worker and client. While self-report tools, such as the one in the example provided in Figure 9.2, can provide information on the topics addressed or covered in each session, the ordering of content across sessions, or the duration of sessions with a client or clients; they are less successful at capturing the quality or spirit of the intervention's delivery.

If you are concerned, for example, that the assessments are not being done with a high degree of quality, you may need some other sort of fidelity data to monitor that particular dimension of the intervention. If you were to add, say, audiotaping of the home visit where an assessment was being conducted with mom and dad, we might be able to pick up on any problems that could be occurring in terms of the way that the assessment is being conducted. Perhaps mom is answering most of the questions for dad, and the home visitor is really using mom's assessment for both parents. Perhaps the home visitor is uncomfortable asking dad certain questions about his risk for violence and tends to move quickly through those questions on the assessment. There might be a lot of things going on that could reduce the potency of the intervention that are also unlikely to come to light if we simply relied on self-report.

Despite its limitations, there are some real benefits to using self-report rather over observation. First, from a teaching perspective, there is value in having someone who is learning something new reflect on their own practice. Learning how to self-critique, and make adjustments accordingly, is an important skill for social workers. Also, using more objective measures such as direct observation or recordings requires additional time and resources. In some cases it may make sense to use these more time and resource intensive approaches to skill someone up in an intervention, but then switch to self-reporting or only occasional observation to check whether the intervention is maintained with a high degree of fidelity.

The right answer is not always obvious, and in reality, there is very little research evidence available to speak to what approach is best. Even for ESI with very well-established protocols around monitoring fidelity, it's hard to say what is required over the long haul to make sure that fidelity is maintained.

Some approaches to fidelity measurement may be less focused on the specific content of the intervention. For example, in Dads Matter-HV, we direct home visitors in the use of assessments with both mothers and fathers, and for the most part, the Dads Matter-HV fidelity instrument is focused on rating whether certain content was delivered. However, other fidelity instruments may be less focused on provided specific content, but rather are founded on particular philosophies and values. So fidelity may be assessed by practitioners' alignment with certain attitudes and beliefs, or the "spirit" of a particular intervention rather than a concrete activity or components. For example, home visitors who used Dads Matter-HV would ideally use a family systems approach to their work with families. Meaning, they would see their client as the family rather than the mom or the dad. This is a pretty abstract concept—one that might be captured by asking home visitors to report their alignment with the philosophy or might be more easily assessed by observing the way that they interact with families. For these reasons, some approaches to the measurement of fidelity include combinations of several of these elements and utilize self-reports as well as multiple observers.

Creating Your Own Fidelity Instrument

Ideally, the intervention that you are using already has a fidelity tool, or tools, that you can use in practice. However, in some cases you may need to create your own fidelity tools and approaches, either because the intervention you are using does not have one, or because you are building your own intervention, or because you are making adaptations to an existing intervention that includes the addition of components that are not measured by the existing fidelity instrument.

Creating your own fidelity instruments is similar to creating a survey, a scale, or another type of measurement instrument. It requires thinking carefully about which elements of the intervention you want to measure and then crafting items on your fidelity measurement tool that elicit insight as to whether an intervention user is indeed using the intervention as you want them too.

To craft a successful fidelity instrument, you need to have substantial knowledge about the intervention and its components. If you are seeking to create a fidelity tool from an existing intervention, you will need to examine the manual, curriculum, or other materials that direct what the user of the intervention actually does with the client. To create a strong fidelity tool, the components of the intervention itself need to be well understood—so it makes a lot of sense to work with the intervention developer, if possible, or consult with an expert in the intervention if you yourself are not highly adept in its use. It also makes a lot of sense to consult with someone who is experienced in creating fidelity instruments or measurement instruments in general.

We would suggest starting with a list of the components of the intervention that are essential to the intervention. Figure 9.5 provides an outline of possible intervention components that might be assessed through a fidelity instrument. The fidelity tool might seek to answer any, some, or all of the questions under each component. You can choose to organize clinical, or procedural, components by session, module, or chapter depending on how the intervention is structured and articulated. You might also select other components that are

---

1. Procedural Content and Quality
   A. Is the user employing the procedures specified by the intervention?

   B. How well is the user employing the intervention elements?

   C. Is the user employing procedures outside of, or counter to, the intervention?

2. Ordering and Dosage
   A. Are the intervention procedures used in the correct order?

   B. Are the procedures used for the correct amount of time?

   C. Are the procedures used with adequate frequency?

3. Population and Problem Match
   A. Is the intervention being used with the appropriate population (race, gender, age, cognitive capacity, etc.)?

   B. Is the intervention being used to address the appropriate problem or goal (diagnosis, symptom, skill, or outcome)?

4. Practitioner and Organization Supports
   A. Does the practitioner have the appropriate educational background and experience to provide the intervention?

   B. Has the practitioner received appropriate training and supervision in the intervention?

   C. Does the organization provide prescribed booster training, supervision, and other supports for the intervention?

Figure 9.5 Possible components of a fidelity instrument.

continuously assessed. As in the previous examples, these components might include specific procedures, or the content of the intervention, or the quality or spirit of the intervention, or both. In addition, fidelity instruments may include information about the situations in which the intervention is used. For example, an intervention may be appropriate for use with adults, but not children. Or an intervention may work well for depression but is not designed to address anxiety. So fidelity instruments may also assess the match between the intervention and population or the intervention and the problem or goal that the practitioner is seeking to address.

As you think about the critical components of the intervention are, you will want to think about the goals of your fidelity instrument as well. Consider how much time is reasonable for either practitioners, supervisors, trainers or observers to spend completing and reviewing the fidelity tool. Also, think about how the information will be used. Will it be used primarily to assess whether someone has been adequately trained in the intervention? Will it be used to guide supervision and booster training? Will it be used to determine the overall "quality" of implementation in a team, or organization? Or, perhaps, it will serve all of these purposes. It is possible that some portions of the fidelity instrument are used for training purposes, while other parts, or perhaps a briefer version of the instrument, are used to monitor ongoing quality and guide regular supervision.

At this point you may find that you have way too many components listed, and it is not realistic for a practitioner to regularly complete the instrument. The goal is to balance comprehensiveness and accuracy, with ease of use and low burden for the user. It can be helpful to look at other examples of how other interventions have organized their fidelity measures, particularly interventions that are in the same "family" as the one you are working on. For example, if you are developing a fidelity instrument for a new peer support group for homeless adolescents, you might look at fidelity instruments that have been developed for other peer support interventions, interventions that target homeless populations, and group interventions. It's generally easier to pull ideas and examples from existing instruments than to build an instrument from the ground up.

It can also be helpful to consult with someone who has created a fidelity instrument before or has experience building similar instruments, such as brief surveys. Constructing a fidelity instrument is deceptively simple, and it can be quite challenging to write questions or items that accurately capture what you are trying to measure.

Once you have constructed your tool, you will want to pilot test it with the same type of folks who will be using the instrument in practice. For example, if you are using the fidelity tool with caseworkers to measure their adherence to a particular casework model, you would want to test it with them and solicit their feedback on how long it took them to complete the instrument, how easy they felt it was to use, and any suggestions that they have for improvement. If possible, it's also helpful to see if the instrument can successfully distinguish between people who are experienced and well-trained in your intervention and those who are not. Do the answers given by practitioners who are good at the intervention and highly familiar with it look different than those who have not had any training in the intervention? If the instrument cannot distinguish between these two groups, then it will be unlikely to provide you with the information you need to ensure that people are well trained in the intervention and are actually applying the intervention as intended in practice.

Overall, taking the time to carefully consider your approach to fidelity is a critical step to implementing a high-quality intervention. Although each approach includes different strengths and drawbacks, some approach to fidelity is needed to help ensure that the intervention is being delivered as you intend. Without a fidelity check, we risk interventions drifting away from their original design or questioning the efficacy of an intervention when the problem is actually one of poor implementation.

Discussion Questions

1. Why is it critical to measure fidelity to interventions in practice?
2. What are the benefits and limitations of using self-report versus observational approaches to monitoring fidelity?
3. Why might an intervention developer insist on using videotaping with a minimum number of clients to ensure fidelity to their model?

10

Conclusion

Overview

In this book we have provided an overview of the process model of evidence-based practice (EBP), highlighting the three-circle model as well as the steps of the process. This process includes asking a research question, finding the best available research evidence, and integrating this research evidence with other important pieces of information related to clients, communities, resources, and the service context. We also reviewed the criteria required to be met for an intervention to be declared an evidence-supported intervention (ESI), and how to find one, and generally assess the quality of intervention research. Implementation, also a step in the EBP process, was also explored, including a review of some of the model approaches to implementing high-quality interventions in practice. We also walked through the adaptation process, including the important step of determining whether an adaptation to an intervention is needed. Finally, we examined the various approaches to ensuring that interventions are implemented as intended using fidelity tools and strategies.

When we began this book, we described how new EBP, and particularly implementation science, is to the field of social work and allied disciplines. These ideas and approaches continue to evolve. In this last chapter we discuss a few exciting developments in EBP and implementation science to highlight what we see as future trends in these areas including *common elements*, online training, and supports for ESI.

Common Elements

The common elements model of EBP is one of the newest approach to EBP and has been developed by Bruce Chorpita and his colleagues (Chorpita & Daleiden, 2009; Chorpita, Daleiden, & Weisz, 2005). This approach to EBP addresses some of the concerns in the field about the inflexibility of ESIs. The common elements approach is based on the idea that ESIs often share many components in common. Other folks have described similar ideas such as Embry and Biglan's (2008) "evidence-based kernels." However, Chorpita and Daleiden's model has been developed the furthest in terms of translation into practice tools and approaches, and so we will highlight this work here in particular.

If you are a more experienced practitioner who has been working in a particular area for a while—say, perhaps home visiting—you might learn about lots of different home-visiting models. There is the Nurse Family Partnership, Parents as Teachers, Early Head Start, and many others. If you get training or gain experience in many different home-visiting models you start to notice something— lots of these models have a great deal of content and strategies in common. Most home-visiting models provide parents with information and training about child development, child safety, and specific skills designed to support children's cognitive development. Most home-visiting models connect parents to supportive services, screen mothers for depression, and have other processes and procedures in common. The same is true of other "families" of interventions such as parent training, mentoring programs for youth, anger management, and stress reduction interventions.

To understand this model, it is helpful to understand how the model was developed. Chorpita, Daleiden, and their colleagues gathered findings from rigorous research studies on the efficacy of child and adolescent mental health interventions over the last 50 or so years. They broke these researched interventions down into smaller, clinically meaningful components. So, for example, when looking at evidence-supported anxiety interventions, many of them include teaching clients how to use relaxation techniques, and so teaching relaxation is one common element. Based on analyses of manuals and research protocols, which described the clinical components of interventions in detail, they found that the most effective interventions are built from only about 80 to 90 common elements and that about 35 or so are the most commonly used elements across programs. So, you might ask, why not train social workers who will be serving children with mental health problems in these 35 effective elements so that they can learn to use them to flexibly treat a variety of behavioral health problems as needed? This is a pretty innovative idea and quite a departure from the approach reflected in the ESI model wherein practitioners are trained on whole, multielement, manualized interventions. After reading this book, and perhaps based on your own experience, you now know that many of these manualized ESI are expensive and hard to maintain in the context of staff turnover, limited resources, and the tendency for interventions to drift away from delivery as intended. Furthermore, the current array of ESI are still limited in terms of their ability to meet the needs of the diverse groups served by social workers.

This common elements idea is just starting to catch on across a variety of settings and is not frequently taught to practitioners as an approach to clinical social work practice. However, in our experience with both students and social workers in the field, the concept is highly appealing, and some research suggests that the common elements approach can be even more effective at achieving outcomes for clients than traditional manualized ESI (Weisz et al., 2012).

You might notice that we don't list challenges for this particular model of EBP. Honestly, it is a bit too new to be sure. We will need some more research and application of the model before any generalizations can be made about its use or the challenges therein. There is some critique out there, however, particularly from intervention developers who feel that interventions are more than the sum of their parts. By taking interventions down to their clinical components, they say, the common elements approach compromises the internal logic of ESI. Remember our story about motivational interviewing? If you aren't doing it correctly, you aren't likely to get good results. There are lots of important considerations when thinking about the internal logic of any intervention. For example, how do you know which element should be done first and for how long or how frequently? Also, there are theoretical and value orientations that contribute to the spirit or style of an intervention that is likely lost with a common elements approach. The jury is still out. These are largely differences of opinion and perspective to date.

Online Training and Support for ESI

Throughout this book we have described the challenges involved in broadly disseminating ESI. Once an intervention produces research findings that indicate it is effectiveness, an important next step is to make the intervention available to the field. Unfortunately, in-person trainings are often expensive and cannot be easily provided to large numbers of organizations. This is especially true for social service agencies that may have little funding for staff training and development and need to bill for services to support their staff. For rural communities, the expense and difficulty in accessing high-quality training is further amplified.

One solution to this problem is to increase the use of online training platforms to disseminate ESIs. For example, many ESI have a training schedule that often includes an initial in-person training for one to three days. The training often includes expenses related to travel for either the participant or trainer and requires that staff are pulled away from service delivery for this time. By translating the initial in-person training for ESI to an online platform, larger numbers of practitioners can receive initial training in the intervention at a relatively low cost, and the training can still be complemented with consultation and booster sessions and other elements needed to support high-quality fidelity and implementation.

Online training for professional development is increasingly common in social work. Each year new social work programs that offer master's and doctoral degrees in social work fully online. Social workers are likely to become increasingly comfortable with these platforms, and their potential for cost-savings seems likely to further increase their use. Furthermore, studies indicate that high-quality online professional education can be as effective as in-person training (e.g., McCutcheon, Lohan, Raynor, & Martin, 2015), particularly when it is interactive in nature (Leszczyński et al., 2018) and combined with proper supports and support material (Childs, Blenkinsopp, Hall, & Walton, 2005). Technology allows for virtual observation and Web meeting–based consultation as well. Social workers trained in ESI in the future may be able to receive training and certification in gold standard ESIs completely through their computers, or even smart phones.

Despite the promise, there are many online training opportunities, professional development programs, and degrees available online that vary in quality. The key the success of these opportunities seems likely reflective of the quality of the program. Still many ESIs are only ready for dissemination via traditional platforms, and when this training becomes available you will have to take the time to make sure whatever training you are investing in is worth the time and costs—both in terms of the quality and utility of the intervention, as well as the quality and utility of the online training.

Continuous Learning Approaches

A great deal of the research emphasis in the EBP movement has been on the development of effectiveness studies aimed at establishing whether a highly specified intervention works under usual practice conditions. A long and resource intensive process of intervention development usually proceeds through a series of stages that includes preliminary studies that inform the intervention, pilot studies of the newly designed intervention, and progressing on to larger quasi-experimental or randomized controlled designs with a high degree of internal validity, ideally replicated in many different communities with many different clients. This is an arduous process. The Dads Matter-HV intervention, which we have highlighted in this book, is the product of 10 years of research and development and has just progressed through its first randomized controlled trial. This is a long time to wait and has been a source of frustration to those in the field who are hoping for evidence-supported father-engagement interventions.

Some might argue that practice-based evidence approaches are a better strategy for using research evidence to guide practice. When we were being trained as master's level social workers, we were trained in single-subject design studies with the idea that individual practitioners could and should evaluate interventions and client outcomes using these designs and produce evidence for the field through these efforts via reports or published manuscripts. This effort has largely fallen to the wayside, although some social work programs may still use this training approach. This change has likely been due in part to the limitations of using this design as well as the many barriers master's level practitioners face when attempting to disseminate their work. The design is a challenge to use in practice when you may only see a client once or twice, the targeted outcome changes over time, outcomes are difficult to measure, or impacts are slow to emerge.

There are, however, other models that can be used to develop practice-based research evidence to good effect, even while integrating currently best available research. One we would like to highlight here is the Breakthrough Series Collaborative (BSC) (Kilo, 1998). The BSC was developed as an approach to improving healthcare quality and integrated both existing research evidence as well as practice-based evidence. It is best suited for solving difficult problems in complex systems—which, of course, are very common in social work. The BSC is a continuous learning approach that begins with the creation of a Collaborative Change Framework. The Collaborative Change Framework is created using the best available research evidence to create targets for change along with expert input.

For example, if the goal of your child welfare agency is to improve the prevention of child maltreatment so that kids do not need to enter the system to begin, you know that parent training interventions are an effective strategy for reducing child maltreatment risk among families. So, one strategy articulated in your Collaborative Change Framework may be to implement an evidence-supported parent training program. But this isn't the only approach that is likely really make a change in your community. You may also know that one of the biggest risk factors for entry into child welfare is lack of resources. So, another strategy may be to create a better network of safety net providers in community from housing, employment, human services, and faith-based community resources that provide aid to families. There aren't RCT data necessarily supporting a specific type of collaboration, but this approach is still supported by the research evidence.

In this model, the research evidence alongside community knowledge and experience is assessed, discussed, and organized by experts in research, service provision, and service receipt. Clients and community participants are just as critical to the creation of a BSC. This group forms a leadership team that not only creates the Collaborative Change Framework, but carries it out while tracking *metrics*, or small outcomes that can be easily measured to determine if the desired change appears to be underway. The group meets together to test out the strategies articulated in the framework and also meets with other leadership teams who are working toward a similar goal to share learning and provide mutual support. So, the research evidence may suggest a particular parent training model is ideal, but after a small test of this model, it may be determined that adaptations are needed to improve its success. Under this model, those changes are proposed, the team members apply the adaptations, and the group comes back together to assess whether the metrics indicate they are moving in the right direction. It is an iterative and ongoing process.

The BSC is not the only continuous learning model available to the field of social work, but it is one that holds some promise in providing a structure to assessing, applying and integrating research evidence with other sources of data and expertise, and it offers some more flexibility than approaches that instruct practitioners to select and apply an intervention off the shelf with a high degree of fidelity to the original model.

Conclusion

As we reflect on some of the most exciting developments in EBP and implementation science, the common thread here may be one of efforts to improve the flexibility of EBP. The common elements approach breaks down complex interventions into their common, high-quality parts and provides practitioners with the tools and structures to apply them in new and adaptive ways. Online platforms can help break our current reliance on in-person training that has been a major barrier to practitioners' access to training in high quality ESIs. Continuous learning approaches, such as the BSC, provide space for both traditional research evidence on the effectiveness of interventions but also explicitly includes client and community participation as well as opportunities to adapt interventions and create interventions collaboratively. The use EBP has nearly constantly elevated discussions about the balance between ensuring quality while allowing for flexibility. Our observation is that the current push seems toward increasingly flexible approaches. However, more research is needed on this balance. We still know very little about how much adaptation most ESIs can tolerate before they are compromised. The use of the BSC is relatively new and hasn't been used in many social work contexts. There is a lot to learn. But it is an exciting and creative time in both EBP and implementation science. We look forward to learning what comes next. We hope you do too.

Discussion Questions

1. Why is important to balance fidelity and quality when engaging in EBP?
2. What other pieces of the implementation process might be supported by technology?
3. What is the advantage to using local data to inform EBP as outlined in the BSC model?

RECOMMENDED TEXTBOOKS ON ASSESSMENT AND EVIDENCE-BASED PRACTICE

Assessment

Corcoran, J., & Walsh, J. (2016). *Clinical assessment and diagnosis in social work practice* (3rd ed.). New York, NY: Oxford University Press.

Jordan, C., & Franklin, C. (2016). *Clinical assessment for social workers: Quantitative and qualitative methods* (4th ed.). Chicago, IL: Lyceum Books.

Pomeroy, E. (2015). *The clinical assessment workbook: Balancing strengths and differential diagnosis* (2nd ed.). Boston, MA: Cengage Learning.

Probst, B. (2015). *Critical thinking in clinical assessment and diagnosis.* Essential Clinical Social Work Series. New York, NY: Springer.

Evidence-Based Practice

Gambrill, E. (1999). Evidence-based practice: An alternative to authority-based practice. *Families in Society, 80*(4), 341–350.

Gambrill, E. (2018). *Critical Thinking and the Process of Evidence-Based Practice.* New York, NY: Oxford University Press.

Gibbs, L. E. (2003). *Evidence-based practice for the helping professions: A practical guide with integrated multimedia.* Pacific Grove, CA: Brooks/Cole-Thomson Learning.

Haynes, R. B., Sackett, D. L., Richardson, W. S., Rosenberg, W., & Langley, G. R. (1997). Evidence-based medicine: How to practice & teach EBM. *Canadian Medical Association. Journal, 157*(6), 788.

Rubin, A., & Bellamy, J. L. (2012). *Practitioner's Guide to Using Research for Evidence-Based Practice.* Hoboken, NJ: Wiley.

Appendix B

EVIDENTIARY CHECKLISTS

Gibbs, L. E. (2013). Quality of Study Rating Form (QSRF): An instrument for synthesizing evaluation studies. *Journal of Social Work Education, 25,* 55–67.

Critical Appraisals Skills Programme (CASP): https://casp-uk.net/casp-tools-checklists/

Centre for Evidence-Based Medicine (CEBM): https://www.cebm.net/2014/06/critical-appraisal/

Grading of Recommendations, Assessment, Development and Evaluations (GRADE): https://bestpractice.bmj.com/info/us/toolkit/learn-ebm/what-is-grade/

Appendix C

GLOSSARY

Adopted Selection of an evidence-supported intervention (ESI) by a an individual practitioner or organization.

Clinical Tailoring Tailoring where clinical judgment, experience, and knowledge are used to make adjustments to treatments based on individual characteristics.

Clinical Techniques Techniques that comprise the technical aspects of providing an intervention or services in social work practice on the micro level.

Common Factors Factors that are broadly reflected in successful interventions regardless of model or theoretical orientation. Acknowledges the role of the clinical content, values, and techniques included in an intervention but underscores the importance of other factors.

Concurrent Validity Shows an association of your measure with other similar and well established measures (such as the Beck Anxiety Inventory).

Construct Validity Degree to which the measurement of a construct accurately reflects the hypothesized structure of the construct and/or the ability of the measurement to uniquely distinguish one construct other constructs.

Content Validity When experts in the field of the construct being measured agree that the items on the scale or in a measurement questionnaire cover the construct or subject matter measured.

Control Group This is the group that does not get the intervention or receives treatment as usual.

Core Elements The clinical elements of an intervention that fundamentally define the nature of the intervention.

Criterion Validity The degree to which a measurement instrument is associated with an external criterion in the way it is theorized to.

Determinant Frameworks Frameworks that identify determinants—both barriers and enablers—that influence implementation success, and some even specify the relationships between these determinants.

Diffusion What happens when ESIs are spread without any intentional marketing or planning.

Dissemination Is the active and planned sharing of information about ESIs.

Dosage Amount of the intervention delivered to the client or community.

Evaluation Frameworks Frameworks specifically developed to evaluate the outcomes of an implementation effort.

Expectancy The client's knowledge that they are receiving treatment and have some expectation for improvement.

Extratherapeutic Factors Individual and environmental factors that are part of the client or the clients' environment that do not relate to the intervention or the provider.

Face Validity Items on a measurement scale make sense in describing the construct of interest.

Factorial Validity For statistical analyses that assess whether the items in a scale measure the same number of proposed scales or subscales.

Generalizable The degree to which the findings of a study could be applied more broadly to other clients or contexts.

History Contemporaneous events, or what happens during the course of the delivery of an intervention that could have been responsible for the change in the outcome variable.

Implementation Systematic application of purposeful activities to bring an ESI to full scale with regard to quality and effectiveness in real practice settings.

Known Groups A method of testing a measurement scale using a group that you know has a particular trait that you're trying to measure and determining whether the scale can correctly discern those with the trait from those without the trait.

Maturation Improvement in an outcome due natural processes such as growing or developing.

Passage of Time Improvement in an outcome due to the elapse of time.

Peripheral Elements Elements of an intervention that do not define the internal logic, of the intervention.

Predictive Validity An association between a measure with a future event .

Random Assignment Process of creating two comparable groups where each participant has equal chances of being selected into the treatment or the control group.

Scale-up Broadly implement interventions for wide dissemination.

Selection bias When one group in a study has different outcomes because of something other than the intervention, or their chances of being selected into the treatment group or the control group is not equivalent.

Tailoring Adaptation that is intended to address variation at the individual client level.

Targeting Adaptation that is designed to fit the needs of a particular subgroup of clients.

Therapeutic Relationship Includes the client's perception of their therapist as warm, empathic, and accepting as well as the agreement between the client and the practitioner on the tasks and goals of treatment.

REFERENCES

American Medical Association. (2016). Ethical principles of psychologists and code of conduct. Retrieved from https://www.apa.org/ethics/code/

Arroyo, K., Lundahl, B., Butters, R., Vanderloo, M., & Wood, D. S. (2017). Short-term interventions for survivors of intimate partner violence: A systematic review and meta-analysis. *Trauma, Violence, & Abuse, 18*(2), 155–171. doi:10.1177/1524838015602736

Asay, T. P., & Lambert, M. J. (2008). The empirical case for the common factors in therapy: Quantitative findings. In M. A. Hubble, B. L. Duncan, & S. D. Miller (Eds.), *The heart and soul of change: What works in therapy* (pp. 23–55). Washington, DC: American Psychological Association.

Bach-Mortensen, A. M., Lange, B. C., & Montgomery, P. (2018). Barriers and facilitators to implementing evidence-based interventions among third sector organisations: a systematic review. *Implementation Science, 13*(1), 103.

Backer, T. E. (2001). *Finding the balance: Program fidelity and adaptation in substance abuse prevention.* Rockville, MD: Center for Substance Abuse Prevention, Substance Abuse and Mental Health Services Administration.

Bagner, D. M., & Eyberg, S. M. (2003). Father involvement in parent training: When does it matter? *Journal of Clinical and Adolescent Psychology, 32*(4), 599–605.

Barrera, M., Castro, F. G., Strycker, L. A., & Toobert, D. J. (2013). Cultural adaptations of behavioral health interventions: A progress report. *Journal of Consulting and Clinical Psychology, 81*(2), 196–205.

Beidas, R., Mehta, T., Atkins, M., Solomon, B., & Merz, J. (2013). Dissemination and implementation science: Research models and methods. In J. Comer & P. Kendall (Eds.), *The Oxford handbook of research strategies for clinical psychology.* New York, NY: Oxford University Press. Retrieved from https://www.oxfordhandbooks.com/view/10.1093/oxfordhb/9780199793549.001.0001/oxfordhb-9780199793549-e-005

Bellamy, J. L. (2009). A national study of male involvement among families in contact with the child welfare system. *Child Maltreatment,14*(3), 255–262.

Bellamy, J. L., Bledsoe, S. E., Mullen, E. J., Fang, L., & Manuel, J. (2008). Learning from agency-university partnership for evidence-based practice in social work: Participant voices from the BEST project. *Journal of Social Work Education, 44*(3), 55–75.

Bellamy, J. L. Spring, B., Mullen, E. J., Satterfield, J. M., Newhouse, R. P., & Ferguson, M. (2013). Implementing evidence-based practice education in social work: A transdisciplinary approach. *Research on Social Work Practice, 23*(4), 426–436.

Blase, K. A., Van Dyke, M., Fixsen, D. L., & Bailey, F. W. (2012). Implementation science: Key concepts, themes and evidence for practitioners in educational psychology. In B. Kelly & D. F. Perkins (Eds.), *Handbook of implementation science for psychology in education* (pp. 13–34). Cambridge, UK: Cambridge University Press.

Castro, F., Barrera, M., & Martinez, C. (2004). The cultural adaptation of prevention interventions: Resolving tensions between fidelity and fit. *Prevention Science, 5*(1), 41–45.

Castro, F. G., Barerra, M., & Steiker Holleran, L. K. (2010). Issues and challenges in the design of culturally adapted evidence-based interventions. *Annual Review of Clinical Psychology, 6*(1), 213–239. doi:10.1146/annurev-clinpsy-033109-132032

Caza, M. (2010). Final report: Evaluation of the mental health first aid training in First Nations communities in Alberta. *Mental Health First Aid Canada*. Retrieved from http://www.mentalhealthfirstaid.ca/EN/about/Documents/Health_Canada_MHFA%20Evaluation%202010.pdf

Childs, S., Blenkinsopp, E., Hall, A., & Walton, G. (2005). Effective e-learning for health professionals and students—barriers and their solutions: A systematic review of the literature—findings from the HeXL project. *Health Information and Libraries Journal, 22*(Suppl. 2), 20–32.

Chorpita, B. F., & Daleiden, E. L. (2009). Mapping evidence-based treatments for children and adolescents: Application of the distillation and matching model to 615 treatments from 322 randomized trials. *Journal of Consulting and Clinical Psychology, 77*(3), 566.

Chorpita, B. F., Daleiden, E. L., & Weisz, J. R. (2005). Identifying and selecting the common elements of evidence based interventions: A distillation and matching model. *Mental Health Services Research, 7*(1), 5–20.

Clara, F., Garcia, K. Y., & Metz, A. (2017). Implementing evidence-based child welfare: The New York City experience. *Casey Family Programs*. Retrieved from https://www.casey.org/evidence-based-child-welfare-nyc/

Cohen, J. (1988). *Statistical power analysis for the behavioral sciences.* (2nd ed.). Hillsdale, NJ: Erlbaum.

Crouch, C., & Parrish, D. E. (2015). Implementing Motivational Interviewing in an urban homeless population: An agency–university collaboration. *Research on Social Work Practice, 25*(4), 493–498. doi:10.1177/1049731514538104

Davis, D. A., Mazmanian, P. E., Fordis, M., Van Harrison, R., Thorpe, K. E., & Perrier, L. (2006). Accuracy of physician self-assessment compared with observed measures of competence: A systematic review. *Journal of the American Medical Association, 296*(9), 1094–1102.

DiClemente, R. J., Davis, T. L., Swartzendruber, A., Fasula, A. M., Boyce, L., Glaude, D., . . . Staples-Horne, M. (2014). Efficacy of an HIV/STI sexual risk-reduction intervention for African American adolescent girls in juvenile detention centers: A randomized controlled trial. *Women & Health, 54*(8), 726–749.

Eccles, M. P., & Mittman, B. S. (2006). Welcome to implementation science. *Implementation Science, 1*, 1. doi:10.1186/1748-5908-1-1

Embry, D. D., & Biglan, A. (2008). Evidence-based kernels: Fundamental units of behavioral influence. *Clinical Child and Family Psychology Review, 11*(3), 75–113.

Fabiano, G. A. (2007). Father participation in behavioral parent training for ADHD: Review and recommendations for increasing inclusion and engagement. *Journal of Family Psychology, 21*(4), 683.

Fabiano, G. A., Pelham, W. E., Cunningham, C. E., Yu, J., Gangloff, B., Buck, M., . . . Gera, S. (2012). A waitlist-controlled trial of behavioral parent training for fathers of children with attention-deficit/hyperactivity disorder. *Journal of Clinical Child and Adolescent Psychology, 41*, 337–345.

Fixsen, D., Blase, K., Metz, A., & Van Dyke, M. (2015). Implementation science. *International Encyclopedia of the Social and Behavioral Sciences, 11*, 695–702.

Fixsen, D., Naoom, S., Blase, K., Friedman, R., & Wallace, F. (2005). *Implementation research: A synthesis of the literature.* Tamps, FL: University of South Florida, Louis de la Parte Florida Mental Health Institute, National Implementation Research Network.

Galano, M. M., Grogan-Kaylor, A. C., Stein, S. F., Clark, H. M., & Graham-Bermann, S. A. (2017). Posttraumatic stress disorder in Latina women: Examining the efficacy of the Moms' Empowerment Program. *Psychological Trauma: Theory, Research, Practice, and Policy, 9*(3), 344–351.

Gambrill. (2018). *Critical thinking and the process of evidence-based practice.* New York, NY: Oxford University Press.

Gearing, R. E., El-Bassel, N., Ghesquiere, A., Baldwin, S., Gillies, J., & Ngeow, E. (2011). Major ingredients of fidelity: A review and scientific guide to improving quality of intervention research implementation. *Clinical Psychology Review, 31,* 79–88.

Gibbs, L. (2003). *Evidence-based practice for the helping professions: A practical guide with integrated multimedia.* Pacific Grove, CA: Brooks/Cole.

Gibbs, L. E. (2013). Quality of Study Rating Form (QSRF): An instrument for synthesizing evaluation studies. *Journal of Social Work Education, 25,* 55–67.

Glasgow, R. E., Vinson, C., Chambers, D., Khoury, M. J., Kaplan, R. M., & Hunter, C. (2012). National Institutes of Health approaches to dissemination and implementation science: Current and future directions. *American Journal of Public Health, 102*(7), 1274–1281. doi:10.2105/AJPH.2012.300755

Glasgow, R. E., Vogt, T. M., & Boles, S. M. (1999). Evaluating the public health impact of health promotion interventions: The RE-AIM framework. *American Journal of Public Health, 89*(9), 1322–1327. doi:10.2105/ajph.89.9.1322

Green-Hennessy, S. (2018). Suspension of the National Registry of Evidence-Based Programs and Practices: The importance of adhering to the evidence. *Substance Abuse Treatment, Prevention, and Policy, 13*(1), 26. doi:10.1186/s13011-018-0162-5

Guterman, N. B., Bellamy, J. L., & Banman, A. (2016). *Parent services log.* Chicago, IL: Author.

Harshbarger, C., Simmons, G., Coelho, H., Sloop, K., & Collins, C. (2006). An empirical assessment of implementation, adaptation, and tailoring: The evaluations of the CDC's national diffusion of VOICES/VOCES. *AIDS Education and Prevention, 18,* 184–197.

Helfrich, C. D., Damschroder, L. J., Hagedorn, H. J., Daggett, G. S., Sahay, A., Ritchie, M., . . . Stetler, C. B. (2010). A critical synthesis of literature on the promoting action on research implementation in health services (PARIHS) framework. *Implementation Science, 5,* 82. doi:10.1186/1748-5908-5-82

Johnson, D. M., & Zlotnick, C. (2009). HOPE for battered women with PTSD in domestic violence shelters. *Professional Psychology, Research and Practice, 40*(3), 234–241. doi:10.1037/a0012519.

Johnson, D. M., Zlotnick, C., & Perez, S. (2011). Cognitive behavioral treatment of PTSD in residents of battered women's shelters: Results of a randomized clinical trial. *Journal of Consulting and Clinical Psychology, 79,* 542–551.

Kaminski, J. W., Valle, L. A., Filene, J. H., & Boyle, C. L. (2008). A meta-analytic review of components associated with parent training program effectiveness. *Journal of Abnormal Child Psychology, 36,* 567–589.

Kilo, C. M. (1998). A framework for collaborative improvement: Lessons from the Institute for Healthcare Improvement's Breakthrough Series. *Quality Management in Health Care, 6*(4), 1–13.

Kitson, A. L., Rycroft-Malone, J., Harvey, G., McCormack, B., Seers, K., & Titchen, A. (2008). Evaluating the successful implementation of evidence into practice using the PARIHS framework: Theoretical and practical challenges. *Implementation Science, 3,* 1. doi:10.1186/1748-5908-3-1

Kreuter, M., & Skinner, C. (2000). Tailoring: What's in a name? *Health Education Research, 15,* 1–4.

Kubany, E. S., Hill, E. E., & Owens, J. A. (2003). Cognitive trauma therapy for battered women with PTSD: Preliminary findings. *Journal of Traumatic Stress, 16,* 81–91.

Kubany, E. S., Hill, E. E., Owens, J. A., Iannce-Spencer, C., McCraig, M. A., & Tremayne, K. J. (2004). Cognitive trauma therapy for battered women with PTSD (CTT-BW). *Journal of Consulting and Clinical Psychology, 72,* 3–18.

Kubany, E. S., & Watson, S. B. (2002). Cognitive trauma therapy for formerly battered women with PTSD: Conceptual bases and treatment outlines. *Cognitive and Behavioral Practice, 9*(2), 111–127.

Leszczyński, P., Gotlib, J., Kopański, Z., Wejnarski, A., Świeżewski, S., & Gałązkowski, R. (2018). Analysis of Web-based learning methods in emergency medicine: Randomized controlled trial. *Archives of Medical Science, 14*(3), 687–694.

Love, S. M., Koob, J. J., & Hill, L. E. (2007). Meeting the challenge of evidence-based practice: Can mental health therapists evaluate their practice? *Brief Treatment and Crisis Intervention, 7,* 184–193.

Lundahl, B. W., Tollefson, D., Risser, H., & Lovejoy, M. C. (2007). A meta-analysis of father involvement in parent training. *Research on Social Work Practice, 18,* 97–106.

Martino, S., Ball, S. A., Gallon, S. L., Hall, D., Ceperich, S., Farentinos, C., . . . Hausotter, W. (2006). *Motivational interviewing assessment: Supervisory tools for enhancing proficiency.* Salem, OR: Northwest Frontier Addiction Technology Transfer Center, Oregon Health and Science University.

McCutcheon, K., Lohan, M. T., Raynor, M., & Martin, D. (2015). A systematic review evaluating the impact of online or blended learning vs. face-to-face learning of clinical skills in undergraduate nurse education. *Journal of Advanced Nursing, 71*(2), 255–270.

Merzel, C., & D'Afflitti, J. (2003). Reconsidering community-based health promotion: Promise, performance, and potential. *American Journal of Public Health, 93*(4), 557–574. doi:10.2105/ajph.93.4.557

Metz, A., & Bartley, L. (2015). Co-creating the conditions to sustain the use of research evidence in public child welfare. *Child Welfare, 94*(2), 115–139.

Metz, A., Bartley, L., Ball, H., Wilson, D., Naoom, S., & Redmond, P. (2015). Active implementation frameworks for successful service delivery: Catawba County Child Wellbeing Project. *Research on Social Work Practice, 25*(4), 415–422. doi:10.1177/1049731514543667

Metz, A., & Louison, L. (2018). *The hexagon tool: Exploring context.* Chapel Hill, NC: National Implementation Network, Frank Porter Graham Child Development Institute, University of North Carolina at Chapel Hill.

Miles, J., & Shevlin, M. (2001). *Applying regression and correlation: A guide for students and researchers.* London, England: SAGE.

Mills, L. G., & Yoshihama, M. (2002). Training children's service workers in domestic violence assessment and intervention: Research findings and implications for practice. *Children and Youth Services Review, 24*(8), 561–581.

Morris, Z. S., Wooding, S., & Grant, J. (2011). The answer is 17 years, what is the question: Understanding time lags in translational research. *Journal of the Royal Society of Medicine, 104*(12), 510–520. doi:10.1258/jrsm.2011.110180

National Association of Social Workers. (2017). Code of ethics. Retrieved from https://www.socialworkers.org/About/Ethics/Code-of-Ethics/Code-of-Ethics-English

National Implementation Research Network. (2016). [Home page]. http://nirn.fpg.unc.edu/

Nilsen, P. (2015). Making sense of implementation theories, models and frameworks. *Implementation Science, 10*(53), 1–13.

O'Neill, M. (2015). Applying critical consciousness and evidence-based practice decision-making: A framework for clinical social work practice. *Journal of Social Work Education, 51*(4), 624–637. doi:10.1080/10437797.2015.1076285

Panter-Brick, C., Burgess, A., Eggerman, M., McAllister, F., Pruett, K., & Leckman, J. F. (2014). Practitioner review: Engaging fathers—Recommendations for a game change in parenting interventions based on a systematic review of the global evidence. *Journal of Child Psychology and Psychiatry, 55*(11), 1187–1212.

Parrish, D. E., & Rubin, A. (2012), Social workers' orientations toward the evidence-based practice process: A comparison with psychologists and licensed marriage and family therapists, *Social Work, 57*(3), 201–210.

Parrish, D., Springer, D., & Franklin, C. (2015). Standardized assessment measures and computer-assisted technologies for evidence-based practice. In C. J. Jordan & C. Franklin (Eds.), *Clinical assessment for social workers: Quantitative and qualitative methods* (4th ed.) (pp. 81–120). Chicago, IL: Lyceum Books.

Prochaska, J. O., & DiClemente, C. C. (1983). Stages and processes of self-change of smoking: Toward an integrative model of change. *Journal of Consulting and Clinical Psychology, 51*(3), 390–395.

Proctor, E. K., Landsverk, J., Aarons, G., Chambers, D., Glisson, C., & Mittman, B. (2009). Implementation research in mental health services: An emerging science with conceptual, methodological, and training challenges. *Administration and Policy in Mental Health, 36*(1), 24–34. doi:10.1007/s10488-008-0197-4

Proctor, E., Silmere, H., Raghavan, R., Hovmand, P., Aarons, G., Bunger, A., ... Hensley, M. (2011). Outcomes for implementation research: Conceptual distinctions, measurement challenges, and research agenda. *Administration and Policy in Mental Health, 38*(2), 65–76.

Rhule, D. M. (2005). Take care to do no harm: Harmful interventions for youth problem behaviors. *Professional Psychology: Research and Practice, 36*(6), 618–625.

Rogers, E. M. (2003). *Diffusion of innovations.* (5th ed.). New York, NY: Free Press.

Rubin, A., & Babbie, E. (2014). *Research methods for social work* (9th ed.). Boston, MA: Cengage Learning.

Rubin, A., & Parrish, D. (2007). Challenges to the future of evidence-based practice in social work education. *Journal of Social Work Education, 43,* 405–428.

Sackett, D. L., Rosenberg, W. M. C., Gray, J. A. M., Haynes, R. B., & Richardson, W. S. (1996). Evidence-based medicine: What it is and what it isn't. *British Medical Journal, 312,* 71–72.

Sackett, D. L., Richardson, W. S., Rosenberg, W., & Haynes, R. B. (1997). *Evidence-based medicine: How to practice and teach EBM.* (1st ed.). New York: Churchill Livingstone.

Sackett, D. L., Straus, S. E., Richardson, W. S., Rosenberg, W., & Haynes, R. B. (2000). *Evidence-based medicine: How to practice and teach EBM* (2nd ed.). New York: Churchill Livingstone.

Straus, S. E., Richardson, W. S., Glasziou, P., & Haynes, R. B. (2005). *Evidence-based medicine: How to practice and teach EBM* (3rd ed.). New York, NY: Churchill Livingstone.

Straus, S. E., Richardson, W. S., Gasziou, P., & Haynes, R. B. (2011). *Evidence-based medicine: How to practice and teach it* (4th ed.). New York, NY: Churchill Livingstone.

Tabak, R. G., Khoong, E. C., Chambers, D. A., & Brownson, R. C. (2012). Bridging research and practice: Models for dissemination and implementation research. *American Journal of Preventive Medicine, 43*(3), 337–350. doi:10.1016/j.amepre.2012.05.024

Tiano, J., & McNeil, C. (2005). The inclusion of fathers in behavioral parent training: A critical evaluation. *Child & Family Behavior Therapy, 27*(4), 1–28.

Treanor, C. J., Santin, O., Prue, G., Coleman, H., Cardwell, C. R., O'Halloran, P., & Donnelly, M. (2019). Psychosocial interventions for informal caregivers of people living with cancer. *Cochrane Database of Systematic Reviews, 6,* CD009912. doi:10.1002/14651858.CD009912.pub2

Tucker, S. Gross, D., Fogg, L., Delaney, K., & Lapporte, R. (1998). The long-term efficacy of a behavioral parent training intervention for families with 2-year-olds. *Research in Nursing & Health, 21,* 199–210.

Tyler, K. A., Schmitz, R. M., Adams, S. A., & Simons, L. G. (2017). Social factors, alcohol expectancy, and drinking behavior: A comparison of two college campuses. *Journal of Substance Use, 22*(4), 357–364.

Velasquez, M. M., von Sternberg, K. L., Floyd, R. L., Parrish, D., Kowalchuk, A., Stephens, N. S., ... Mullen, P. D. (2017). Preventing alcohol and tobacco exposed pregnancies: CHOICES Plus in primary care. *American Journal of Preventive Medicine, 53*(1), 85–95.

Velasquez, M. M., von Sternberg, K., Stotts, A., Parrish, D., & Kowalchuk, A. Tablet-based intervention to prevent substance-exposed pregnancy in primary care. National Institutes of Health, National Institute on Alcohol Abuse and Alcoholism R01 grant (R01 AA022924).

Wampold, B. E., & Imel, Z. E. (2015). The great psychotherapy debate: The evidence for what makes psychotherapy work. New York, NY: Routledge.

Weisz, J. R., Chorpita, B. F., Palinkas, L. A., Schoenwald, S. K., Miranda, J., Bearman, S. K., . . . Gibbons, R. D.; Research Network on Youth Mental Health. (2012). Testing standard and modular designs for psychotherapy with youth depression, anxiety, and conduct problems: A randomized effectiveness trial. *Archives of General Psychiatry, 69,* 274–282.

Wingwood, G. M., & DiClemente, R. J. (2008). The ADAPT-ITT model: A novel method of adapting evidence-based HIV Interventions. *Journal of Acquired Immune Deficiency Syndromes, 47,* S40–S46.

Zayas, L. H., Bellamy, J. L., & Proctor, E. (2012). Considering the multiple service contexts in cultural adaptations: The case for parenting interventions. In R. Brownson, G. Colditz, & E. Proctor (Eds.), *Dissemination and implementation research in health: Translating science to practice* (pp. 483–497). New York, NY: Oxford.

INDEX

Tables and figures are indicated by *t* and *f* following the page number

For the benefit of digital users, indexed terms that span two pages (e.g., 52–53) may, on occasion, appear on only one of those pages.

ACS (Administration for Children's Services), New York City, 84–88
ACT (assertive community treatment), 76
active comparison group, 27–28
Active Implementation Frameworks, 68, 77
adaptation plan, 117
adaptation refinement stage, 114*f*, 115
adaptations
    ADAPT-ITT model, 115–17
    alternatives to, 110–12
    challenges to, 99–100
    choosing to use, 101–2, 110–12
    client-related problems, 104–9, 105*t*
    clinical tailoring, 95, 98
    common factors, 98–99, 99*f*
    context-related problems, 109–10
    core elements, 96–98, 97*t*, 120–21, 125
    cultural, 89, 90, 113–15, 114*f*
    defined, 90–91
    efficacy problems, 105*t*, 108–9
    engagement problems, 105*t*, 107–8
    general process
        application to intervention, 124–25
        identification of targets, 120–24
        overview, 118
        specification of problem, 118–19
        testing, 125–26
    internal logic of interventions, 91–92
    mismatch across clients, interventions, and service contexts, 101–2, 102*f*, 103
    overview, 89–90
    participation problems, 105–7, 105*t*
    peripheral elements, 95–96, 97*t*, 121–22
    problems, identifying, 102–4

    research on impact of, 93
    service context problems, 104–9, 105*t*
    targeting and tailoring, 93–98
ADAPT-ITT model, 115–17
adaptive leadership drivers, 78–79
Administration for Children's Services (ACS), New York City, 84–88
adoption, 67
applying adaptations, 124–25
Asay, T. P., 98
assertive community treatment (ACT), 76
assessments, 11–12, 55, 151

Backer, T. E., 90–91
background questions, 38
Barrera, M., 90
bias
    in implementation, 62–63
    in research, 16–17
    selection, 46–47
books on implementation, 72–73
Boolean logic, 43–44
bottom–up model, 5–9
Breakthrough Series Collaborative (BSC), 148–49
buy-in, 11–12, 21, 98, 122

Campbell Collaboration, 15–16, 39
case examples, in self-report instruments, 131
Casey Family Programs, 84–88
Castro, F., 90
CBT (cognitive-behavioral therapy), 28–29
challenges to evidence-supported interventions, 28–33, 33*f*
checklist fidelity instruments, 131–34, 133*f*

child welfare interventions, 84–88, 94
Chorpita, B. F., 144–46
CIAO (client characteristics, intervention being considered, alternative intervention, if any, and outcome), 36
Clara, F., 84–88
clearinghouses of interventions, 14–15, 16–17, 41–42, 42f
client characteristics, intervention being considered, alternative intervention, if any, and outcome (CIAO), 36
client-oriented, practical, evidence-search (COPES), 36
clients
  adaptation problems, 104–9, 105t
  assessments of, 11–12, 55
  buy-in, 11–12, 21, 98, 122
  engagement problems, 105t, 107–8
  integrating critical appraisal of research with, 20–21
  participation problems, 105–7, 105t, 118–19, 126
  selecting intervention for, 53
  in three circle model, 5–6, 6f, 8
  underrepresented groups in research, 29–30
clinical adaptation, 101
clinical tailoring, 95, 124
clinical techniques, 98
coaching for implementation, 74–75
Cochrane Collaboration, 15–16, 39
cognitive-behavioral therapy (CBT), 28–29
Cognitive Trauma Therapy for Battered Women With PTSD (CTT-BW), 56–57, 59–60
Collaborative Change Framework, 148–49
colleagues, consulting about interventions, 14
common elements model of evidence-based practice (EBP), 144–46
common factors, 98–99, 99f
community assessment, 11–12
competency, measuring, 130–31
competency drivers, 77f, 77–78
Conceptual Model of Implementation Research, 69
concurrent validity, 51
conferences, learning about interventions at, 14
construct validity, 51–52
consulting for implementation, 74–75
content validity, 51
context of intervention studies, 30–31
context-related adaptation problems, 109–10
continuous improvement of practice, 22–23
continuous learning approaches, 147–49
control group, 47–48
COPES (client-oriented, practical, evidence-search), 36
core components analysis, 92

core elements, adaptations of, 96–98, 97t, 120–21, 125
correlations, 18–19, 19t
cost-effectiveness, 54
cost planning tools, 71–72
criteria for evidence-supported interventions, 27–28, 28f
criterion validity, 51
critical appraisal of research
  general discussion, 17–20
  measurement of outcome variable, 50–52
  overview, 44–47
  pre-experimental designs, 50
  quasi-experimental designs, 49
  single-system designs, 49–50
  statistical and practical significance, 52–53
  threats to internal validity, 47–49
Crouch, C., 75
CTT-BW (Cognitive Trauma Therapy for Battered Women With PTSD), 56–57, 59–60
cultural adaptation, 89, 90, 113–15, 114f
cultural adaptation trial stage, 114f, 115
cultural competence, 95

Dads Matter-HV intervention
  challenges in implementation, 69–70
  core elements, adaptations of, 96–97
  fidelity instrument, 131–34, 133f, 139–40
  improvements on, 22
  loss of potency from research to practice, 61–62
  Parent Service Log, 131–34, 133f, 135–36
  peripheral elements, adaptations of, 96
Daleiden, E. L., 144–46
databases, online, 39–40, 42–44
decision-making model, 2
determinant frameworks, 67–68
diffusion, 66–67
diffusion of innovations theory, 65–66
dismantling studies, 92
dissemination, 67
diversity in intervention studies, 29–30
dosing, 122
drift, 90–91, 127–28
drivers supporting implementation, 75–79, 77f
dropouts, 105–7, 105t

EBP. See evidence-based practice
effectiveness of interventions, evaluating, 22–23
effectiveness questions, 36–38
effect sizes, 18–20, 19t, 52–53, 61–62
efficacy problems, 105t, 108–9
engagement problems, 105t, 107–8, 118–19, 122
ESIs. See evidence-supported interventions
evaluating research. See critical appraisal of research
evaluation frameworks, 68–69
evaluation of effectiveness of interventions, 22–23

evidence-based practice (EBP). *See also* process
model of evidence-based practice
common elements model, 144–46
evidence-based practices model, 26
history of, 2–4
in medicine versus social work, 2–3
misperceptions about, 23
recommended textbooks on, 151
three circle model, 5–9, 6*f*
training in, 24
evidence-supported interventions (ESIs)
ACS example, 84–88
challenges to, 28–33, 33*f*
criteria for, 27–28, 28*f*
example of search for, 55–60
limitations of, 1–2
online training and support for, 146–47
overview, 26–27
preparing for challenges in selection
of, 60
evidentiary checklists, 45, 153
expectancy, 98, 122
experience, integrating critical appraisal of
research with, 20
expert consultation for adaptations, 117, 120
exploration stage of implementation, 79–80,
81*f*, 84–85
extratherapeutic factors, 98, 123, 125

face validity, 51
factorial validity, 51–52
Families First Prevention Act, 27
fathers, home-visiting intervention for. *See* Dads
Matter-HV intervention
fidelity
ACS example, 87–88
creating instruments, 140–42, 141*f*
defined, 128
importance of, 128–29
loss of potency from research to practice, 63
monitoring, 75, 129
observation, 136–40, 137*f*
overview, 28, 127–28
self-report instruments
benefits and challenges of, 138–40
case examples, 131
checklists, 131–34, 133*f*
competency, 130–31
knowledge of interventions, 130*f*, 130
Likert scales, 135*f*, 135–36
overview, 129–30
five-step model, 5–9
full stage of implementation, 83, 85–86

Garcia, K. Y., 84–88
general adaptation process
application to intervention, 124–25

identification of targets, 120–24
overview, 118
specification of problem, 118–19
testing, 125–26
generalizability, 49–50, 115
Google Scholar
example of search on, 55–56
overview, 40–41
strategies for searching on, 42–44

Helping to Overcome PTSD Through
Empowerment (HOPE), 56, 57–58
"Hexagon: An Exploration Tool, The," 54
history, 47–48
home-visiting models, 145. *See also* Dads Matter-
HV intervention
HOPE (Helping to Overcome PTSD Through
Empowerment), 56, 57–58
housing first framework, 111–12

implementation. *See also* fidelity
ACS example, 84–88
coaching and consulting, 74–75
competency drivers, 77*f*, 77–78
defined, 64–66, 67
factors and drivers that support, 75–79, 77*f*
leadership drivers, 77*f*, 78–79
loss of potency from research to practice,
61–64, 63*f*
manuals, books, or other supporting
materials, 72–73
models of, 67–70
non-ESI interventions, 84
organizational drivers, 77*f*, 78
overview, 21–22, 61
pre-assessment, 71–72
stages of
exploration, 79–80, 81*f*
full implementation, 83
initial implementation, 82–83
installation, 80
overview, 79
supports, tools, and processes, 71*f*, 71–75
terms related to, 66–67
training, 73–74
incentives, 123
Incredible Years (IY), 73, 136
information gathering stage, 113–14, 114*f*
informed consent, 21
initial stage of implementation, 82–83, 85–86
installation stage of implementation, 80, 85
integrating sources of evidence, 20–21, 53–54
internal consistency reliability, 50
internal logic of interventions, 91–92
internal validity, threats to, 45–46, 47–49
interrater reliability, 50
intervention purveyors, 71

interventions. *See also* fidelity; implementation;
     research on interventions
  client collaboration, 6–7
  defined, 2
  evaluation of, 22–23
  lists of effective, 31–33
  loss of potency from research to practice,
     61–64, 63*f*
  resources for, 7–8
  strategies for finding relevant, 14–15
  transparency, 8
  updating, 22–23
IY (Incredible Years), 73, 136

key values of process model, 22*f*
knowledge of interventions, measuring, 130*f*, 130
known groups, 51
Kreuter, M., 94

Lambert, M. J., 98
language adaptations, 114
leadership drivers, 77*f*, 78–79
libraries, researching through, 39–40
Likert scales, 135*f*, 135–36
listening tour, 84–85
lists of effective interventions, 31–33

maintenance, 69, 83
manualization, 28
manuals for implementation, 72–73
Map of the Adaptation Process (MAP), 115–16
Martinez, C., 90
materials for implementation, 72–73
maturation, 48–49
measurement of outcome variable, 50–52
medicine, evidence-based practice in, 2–3
MEP (Moms' Empowerment Program), 56, 58–60
meta-analyses, 39, 46–47
Metz, A., 84–88
MI. *See* motivational interviewing
Mills, L. G., 130–31
misperceptions about evidence-based practice, 23
Moms' Empowerment Program (MEP), 56, 58–60
motivational interviewing (MI)
  fidelity, 14, 63, 75
  fidelity tool, 136–38, 137*f*
  training resources, 63–64
motivation strategies, 122, 123, 125

National Implementation Research
     Network (NIRN)
  ACS partnership, 84–88
  Active Implementation Frameworks, 77
  The Hexagon: An Exploration Tool, 54
  implementation research, 65–66, 68
  stages of implementation
     exploration, 79–80, 81*f*

full, 83
  initial, 82–83
  installation, 80
  overview, 79
National Registry of Evidence-Based Programs
     and Practices, 67
needs assessment, 55
NIRN. *See* National Implementation Research
     Network
non-ESI interventions, 84
no-shows, improving rates of, 76–77

observation
  benefits and challenges of, 138–40
  fidelity monitoring, 136–38, 137*f*
  in training, 74–75
online sources
  clearinghouses, 14–15, 16–17, 41–42, 42*f*
  databases, 39–40, 42–44
  Google Scholar
     example of search on, 55–56
     overview, 40–41
     strategies for searching on, 42–44
  meta-analyses, 39, 46–47
  others, 40–42, 42*f*
  registries, 14–15, 16–17, 41–42, 42*f*, 67
  systematic reviews, 14–17, 39, 46–47
online training and support for evidence-
     supported interventions (ESIs), 146–47
organizational drivers, 77*f*, 78
outcome variable, measurement of, 50–52

Parent–Child Interaction Therapy
     (PCIT), 109
Parent Service Log (PSL), 131–34, 133*f*, 135–36
parent training interventions
  access to interventions, 31–32
  adaptations in, 94–95, 97, 97*t*
  efficacy problems, 108–9
  engagement problems, 107
  general adaptation process
     application to intervention, 124–25
     identification of targets, 120–24
     overview, 118
     specification of problem, 118–19
     testing, 125–26
  participation problems, 106–7
  sharing knowledge with clients, 6–7
participation problems, 105–7, 105*t*, 118–19, 126
passage of time, 48–49
patient, intervention, comparison intervention,
     and outcome (PICO) format, 35–38, 37*f*
PCIT (Parent–Child Interaction
     Therapy), 109
peripheral elements, adaptations of, 95–96, 97–98,
     97*t*, 121–22
personal digital assistants (PDAs), 82–83

PICO (patient, intervention, comparison intervention, and outcome) format, 35–38, 37*f*
pilot tests, 114–15, 117, 125–26, 142
podcasts, Cochrane Collaboration, 39
post-traumatic stress disorder (PTSD) in battered women
  choosing intervention, 59–60
  CTT-BW, 56–57
  HOPE, 56, 57–58
  MEP, 56, 58–59
  needs assessment, 55
  search for interventions, 55–56
practical significance, 52–53
practice-based evidence approaches, 148–49
pre-assessment, 71–72
predictive validity, 51
pre-experimental designs, 50
preliminary adaptation design stage, 114*f*, 114
preliminary adaptation tests stage, 114*f*, 114–15
problem alcohol use interventions, 101–2, 103
processes for implementation, 71*f*, 71–75
process model of evidence-based practice (EBP).
    See also critical appraisal of research; implementation; research on interventions
  assessment, 11–12
  challenges to, 23*f*, 23–25
  integrating sources of evidence, 20–21, 53–54
  key values of, 22*f*
  overview, 10–11, 34–35
  preparing for challenges in ESI selection, 60
  questions, formulating, 11–15, 13*f*, 35–38
  steps in, 11*f*
  three circle model, 5–9
Proctor, E., 69
Promoting Action on Research Implementation in Health, 68
PSL (Parent Service Log), 131–34, 133*f*, 135–36
psychosocial assessment, 11–12
PTSD in battered women. *See* post-traumatic stress disorder in battered women
public libraries, researching through, 39–40
PubMed, 43–44

quality control, 64, 84
quasi-experimental designs, 49
quasi-experimental trials, 27
questions, formulating
  general discussion, 11–15, 13*f*
  PICO format, 35–38, 37*f*

racial and ethnic minorities, 29–30
random assignment, 47
randomized controlled trials (RCTs), 27, 46–47
Reach Effectiveness Adoption Implementation Maintenance (RE-AIM), 68–69

readiness to change, 111–12
recorded observation, 74–75, 136–38
registries of interventions, 14–15, 16–17, 41–42, 42*f*, 67
relationship adaptations, 123–24, 125
reliability, 50
research experts, contacting, 14
research hierarchy for intervention studies, 45, 46*f*
research on interventions. *See also* critical appraisal of research
  databases, 39–40, 42–44
  example of search for, 55–60
  Google Scholar
    example of search on, 55–56
    overview, 40–41
    strategies for searching on, 42–44
  impact of adaptations, 93
  integrating sources of evidence, 20–21, 53–54
  meta-analyses, 39, 46–47
  other online sources, 40–42, 42*f*
  overview, 15–17, 38–39
  registries, 14–15, 16–17, 41–42, 42*f*, 67
  strategies for, 42–44
  systematic reviews, 14–17, 39, 46–47
  in three circle model, 5–6, 6*f*
resources
  context-related adaptation problems, 109
  integrating critical appraisal of research with, 20
  interventions limited by, 32
  in three circle model, 5–8, 6*f*
Rogers, E. M., 65–66
Rubin, A., 36

Sackett, D. L., 2
searching for interventions. *See* research on interventions
search terms, strategies for use of, 42–44
selection bias, 46–47
self-report instruments
  benefits and challenges of, 138–40
  case examples, 131
  checklists, 131–34, 133*f*
  competency, 130–31
  knowledge of interventions, 130*f*, 130
  Likert scales, 135*f*, 135–36
  overview, 129–30
service context adaptation problems, 104–9, 105*t*
simplicity of interventions, 76
single-system designs, 49–50
SIPE (Sustaining and Integrating Preventative EBMs) team, 86
Skinner, C., 94
social justice mandate, 2–3
sources of evidence, integrating, 20–21, 53–54
specification of adaptation
  problem, 118–19

stages of implementation
  exploration, 79–80, 81*f*
  full, 83
  initial, 82–83
  installation, 80
  overview, 79
statistical significance, 18, 52–53
steps in process model. *See also* critical appraisal of
      research; research on interventions
  assessment, 11–12
  evaluation of interventions, 22–23
  evidence, searching for, 15–17
  example of search for intervention, 55–60
  implementing interventions, 21–22
  integrating sources of evidence, 20–21, 53–54
  key values of, 22*f*
  overview of, 11*f*
  preparing for challenges in ESI selection, 60
  questions, formulating, 11–15, 13*f*
supporting materials for implementation, 72–73
supports for implementation, 71*f*, 71–75
sustainability, 86
Sustaining and Integrating Preventative EBMs
      (SIPE) team, 86
systematic reviews, 14–17, 39, 46–47

tailoring adaptations, 93–98
targeting adaptations, 93–98, 120–24
teams of practitioners, use of process model by,
      10, 23–24
technical leadership drivers, 78–79
telephone consultation, 75

telephone intervention, 76–77
testing adaptations, 114–15, 117, 119, 125–26
test–retest reliability, 50
TexShare card, 39–40
theater testing, 117
therapeutic relationship, 98
threats to internal validity, 45–46, 47–49
three circle model, 5–9, 6*f*
tools for implementation, 71*f*, 71–75
training, 24, 73–74, 110–11, 146–47
transparency, 8, 21
true/false questions, 130*f*, 130
truncation, 43
turnover of staff, 87–88

underrepresented groups in research, 29–30

validity
  assessing, 17–20
  concurrent, 51
  construct, 51–52
  content, 51
  criterion, 51
  face, 51
  factorial, 51–52
  measures of, 51–52
  predictive, 51
  threats to internal, 45–46, 47–49

wildcard logic, 43

Yoshihama, M., 130–31